D1247172

OKLAVA

This book is dedicated to my *Nene* (Grandma) Bahire,
for creating so much of my inspiration and forever pleasing
others through your incredible cooking and loving heart.

First published in 2018 by

INTERLINK BOOKS
An imprint of Interlink Publishing Group, Inc.
46 Crosby Street, Northampton, Massachusetts 01060
www.interlinkbooks.com

Text copyright © Selin Kiazim 2018
Design & photography copyright © Octopus Publishing Group, Ltd. 2018
American edition copyright © Interlink Publishing Group, Inc. 2018

All rights reserved. No part of this work may be reproduced or utilized
in any form or by any means, electronic or mechanical, including
photocopying, recording or by any information storage and retrieval
system, without the prior written permission of the publisher.

ISBN 978-1-56656-028-3
Library of Congress Cataloging-in-Publication Data available.

Printed and bound in China

10 9 8 7 6 5 4 3 2 1

Publishing Director: Stephanie Jackson
Art Director: Yasia Williams-Leedham
Design: Grade Design
Cover Design: Julian D. Ramirez
Senior Editor: Alex Stetter
American Edition Editor: Leyla Moushabeck
Photography: Chris Terry
Props Stylist: Cynthia Inions
Senior Production Manager: Peter Hunt

To request our complete 48-page, full-color catalog, please call us toll free at 1-800-238-LINK,
visit our website at www.interlinkbooks.com, or send us an e-mail: info@interlinkbooks.com.

Ovens should be preheated to the specific temperature—if using a fan-assisted oven,
follow manufacturer's instructions for adjusting the time and the temperature.

CONTENTS

INTRODUCTION   6

SALADS & SNACKS   12

SAVORY BAKES   44

MEAT   66

SEAFOOD   114

VEGETABLES & GRAINS   134

DRINKS   162

DRESSINGS, DIPS & THINGS   184

SWEET THINGS   202

INDEX   232

ACKNOWLEDGMENTS   240

SELIN:
FROM THE BEGINNING

Oklava translates simply as "rolling pin." When I think of an *oklava* it always conjures up memories of my *nene* (grandmother): a rolling pin was never far from her hands, which always meant a delicious treat was imminent.

I was born and grew up in north London, surrounded by Turkish and Greek Cypriots. As all immigrant communities seem to do, they'd all settled in one corner of the city. As a result, Turkish grocers were always nearby, which made it very easy for Mom to bring us up on traditional Turkish fare, including dolmas, *yahni yemek*, *köfte*, *böreks* and, of course, kebabs.

My parents went to London from Cyprus in the 1970s, but our ties to the country have always remained strong. My grandparents and cousins are all there, and our family has lived on the island for generations.

Thanks to its strategic location in the eastern Mediterranean, Cyprus has been ruled by many nations and settled by many cultures over the centuries. It has had Greek settlers for thousands of years, and in the early 1500s Turkish settlers (including my ancestors) arrived with the Ottoman Empire. Cyprus, as we now know it, has been peacefully divided in two since 1974, with the Turks living in the north and the Greeks in the south.

There is a huge amount of crossover between Turkish and Greek food. Much of it is practically the same, just with different names: for example, what is *şeftali* to us is *şeftalia* to the Greeks, and *köfte* is *keftedes*. The biggest difference between the two sides is that the Turks are Muslims and therefore do not eat pork, but the recipes are often essentially the same—one version will use lamb and the other pork.

The food of Cyprus is all about island cooking; it's simply what is grown on the land. Of course there are more supermarkets these days and some imports through Turkey, but shopping at the local market or even buying fruit and veg from roadside stalls is still very much how things are done, and in the villages they eat what they grow. Food in Cyprus is immensely seasonal, as I was reminded when looking for cauliflowers in June, while on a photo shoot for this book—there weren't any! And at certain times of the year, the dishes prepared in all the households will be similar. On that trip in June, a lot of the older women, including my grandmother, had black-stained hands from preparing *ceviz macunu*, candied walnuts. Making these is hugely laborious and takes a week. My grandmother doesn't even particularly like candied walnuts; she just makes them for the enjoyment of others!

In comparison to Turkish food with its Middle-Eastern influences, Cypriot cooking is very simple and more Mediterranean. In Turkey, with its history in the spice trade and influences from the Ottoman Empire, they use a lot more spices, as well as more nuts and dried fruits, to produce the most wonderful aromatic dishes, which can be quite rich. Cypriot flavors are simpler, ingredients lists shorter. There are also regional differences, with some areas of Turkey using butter as their main cooking fat and others olive oil.

First steps

In all honesty, I was pretty over Turkish food by the time I turned 19, which is when I enrolled at Westminster Kingsway College to study for a Professional Chef's Diploma. At college I learned the basics of French cooking, which couldn't have been any further from Mom's cooking. I loved my years at college—it was the first time I felt like I was actually good at something. I was certainly never one for academic studies, but I did naturally lean towards the more creative subjects and had always loved to eat, so I guess it was perhaps inevitable that I would end up a chef.

Opposite: *In Cyprus with my grandfather, Kazım Doğramacı, my mother, Pervin Kıazim, and my grandmother, Bahire Doğramacı.*

I started at college thinking I would learn the basics and then perhaps work as a caterer, as I was pretty petrified by the idea of being a chef in a restaurant kitchen in London. Any thoughts of being a caterer quickly disappeared when I found myself completely at home in the college kitchens and immersed in cooking books. It became an obsession, and still is. I approached one of my college lecturers, Vince Cottam, who went on to mentor me through many competitions, including one that was run by the "godfather of fusion" himself, New Zealand-born chef Peter Gordon. Competition day came, and that was the first time I met Peter. I was in my third and final year at college, and until then I had mostly met fairly intimidating head chefs in my work experience. Now I was at the point where I needed to decide what kind of kitchen I wanted to work in. Peter was—and still is—the friendliest chef I have ever come across, and I knew I wanted to work for him.

I won the competition and my prize was a five-week trip to New Zealand to work at some of the country's top restaurants. One of them was Dine by Peter Gordon, in a five-star hotel in Auckland. It was during my time there that Peter offered me the opportunity of a trial at his London restaurant, The Providores. I still clearly remember walking down the stairs to the kitchen for the first time, with Peter singing to me at the top of his voice. I worked a double shift that day and loved every minute of it: everyone in the kitchen was so friendly and made sure I tried as many different flavors as possible. No one shouting? No angry head chef? My mind was blown from day one.

Moving on.
I couldn't have dreamed of a better start to my career: I learned such an incredible amount at The Providores, not only about food, but also about how to interact with fellow team members and create a place where people genuinely wanted to work. Leaving was tough, but I knew I wanted my own restaurant some day, so I had to keep pushing myself

and climbing the ladder. There were no senior positions available at The Providores, so after two years I handed in my notice to Peter, crying my eyes out.

The job I had lined up didn't work out, and three months later I found myself working for Peter again, this time at his Covent Garden restaurant, Kopapa (now closed). After working at Kopapa as a sous chef for a year, I was made head chef. I was pretty confident in my cooking abilities at this point, but had never managed people before, so I found it a tough place to work. Again I learned a lot, mostly about myself and my management style. Kopapa gave me a great insight into what it would take to open a new restaurant and how hard it is to make one successful.

By the end of 2012, my head was bursting with ideas and all I could think about was opening my own restaurant. I decided it was time to move on and try to make a name for myself. Pop-up dinner evenings had become a big thing, so it seemed the natural platform for me to try it out. But before I could launch myself into the cut-throat London food scene, I had to decide what kind of food I wanted to present. I grew up in London, where the culture and the food are so diverse: it is incredibly inspiring to see people from all around the world take the humble cooking from their own countries and modernize it to work in the city. The combination of my classical training at college, my Turkish-Cypriot family (including the time spent with my *nene* in her home village), my north London upbringing, and four years exploring food from around the world with Peter Gordon gave me a great grounding that meant I could bounce off in any direction I wanted, but I hadn't ever really cooked my "own" menu before.

Finding my own way
There were two things that led me to develop my style of modern Turkish cooking. First of all, there's nothing I love to eat more than a well-made kebab: anything cooked

over charcoal just tastes better! Second, I wanted to do something that no one else was doing, which is pretty much impossible, since there's always someone who thought of an idea before you—but that wouldn't stop me trying. I thought to myself, if I want to find something that sets me apart, I need to look at all the elements that make me the chef I am.

Once I finished working at Kopapa, I booked a trip to Istanbul and went in search of inspiration. I was already starting to lean towards more Middle-Eastern flavors in my cooking, and it occurred to me that all anyone thinks of when it comes to Turkish food are kebabs. Turkish food is rich, diverse, and steeped in tradition, but relatively unexplored in the modern cooking world, and that was incredibly exciting for me. Even now, as I write this, we are exploring something new: earlier I was talking to my sous chef Nick about today's market special, a shrimp köfte flatbread with smoked eggplant salad. I told him to mix some lamb suet into the fish köfte mixture and he thought I was slightly insane.

Opening the doors at Oklava

I got lucky while I was doing the pop-ups: after only a short while I was put in touch with the owners of what would become Trip Kitchen and Bar in Haggerston, east London. I spent a six-month residency there and was able to start showcasing the sort of food I wanted to cook. It went very well, but still not enough people knew about what I was doing. Then, one random evening towards the end of my time there, Giles Coren, the food critic for *The Times*, came in for dinner. To say I was petrified is a slight understatement; I immediately started doubting every dish on the menu, thinking he was going to hate everything and completely annihilate me. Somehow I managed to calm down, remember the faith I had in all my dishes, and just cook to the best of my ability. It paid off, because he gave my food a glowing—if not perfect—review. I was gobsmacked. The review meant that I could leave Trip Kitchen on a massive high, with

the confidence of knowing that if I could just get to the point of opening my own place, I would certainly be in a position to compete with other London restaurants.

In the end it took just over 18 months to open the doors at Oklava. There were many opportunities along the way but nothing quite worked out, which made this phase of my life an incredibly frustrating time. I kept myself going with the occasional pop-up or event while searching for a site, funding, and the right business partner. One of those events was a guest chef appearance at Salt Yard Group's Ember Yard in Soho. I didn't know it at the time, or even meet her then, but their operations manager, Laura Christie, would eventually become my business partner.

A few months passed before Laura and I met up to discuss the possibility of starting a restaurant together. This may sound like a cliché, but I knew immediately that Laura was just the person I was looking to partner up with. She is passionate about the industry, knowledgeable about service and wine, and great at all the things I'm not good at—and she loves a good Excel spreadsheet. I knew I wanted the restaurant to explore Turkish wines, and Laura not only expressed an interest in Middle-Eastern wines, but also, like me, wanted to do something with a wine list that no one else was doing. From that point on, we developed Oklava into what it is now.

This book brings together recipes that reflect my cooking style, inspired by my grandmother and mother. Some are a little complex—these are the Oklava dishes— but you will also find my versions of simple, traditional family recipes. I hope you will enjoy cooking from this book, or even using it as inspiration for your own dishes. Please don't just look at the pictures—I want to see grubby pages because you have been using this book so much!

LAURA:
MAKING IT WORK

When I first met Selin during my time at Salt Yard Group, I immediately knew she was someone I wanted to work with. As well as being fantastically talented, she had a clear vision of what she wanted to achieve and shared a lot of my own passions—not just the amazing produce and wine we are lucky enough to work with at Oklava, but also a real love of the restaurant industry. Knowing at that point very little about Turkish food, wine, or culture, but realizing this was a special opportunity, I was quick to express my interest and we have been working together ever since.

From the beginning, we both felt it made sense to have a Turkish drinks list for a Turkish restaurant, and we set about researching what was available. With the help of friend and colleague Melisa Atay, herself the daughter of Turkish wine producers, we were introduced to some wineries and packed ourselves off to Istanbul to meet them.

This was my first time in Turkey and I had mixed feelings about our plan, having told everyone we were putting together an exclusively Turkish wine list and receiving some pretty shocked feedback. On arriving in Istanbul I was amazed to see that almost every restaurant's wine list was dominated not by Old World or even international producers, but by home-grown Turkish wineries. For those who have not had the pleasure of discovering Istanbul's dining scene, we are talking about some seriously impressive restaurants. We were lucky enough to meet some of the producers we now proudly list on our menu: Diren, Arcadia, Büyülübag, and Paşaeli, to name a few. The passion, innovation, and attention to detail shown by all of these wineries are second to none. It was an inspirational trip, and cemented our belief that Oklava was the perfect platform for modern Turkish wine. It suited our "bring Turkish food to the London foodie" concept to a tee.

Keen to make sure this wasn't purely a rose-tinted vision (or perhaps a rosé-tinted one), we organized a

tasting back home and were pleased to discover we had some diverse and delicious options for our list. Turkey is one of the oldest wine-growing areas in the world and has some brilliant producers, but, rather boringly, a combination of administrative red tape and very healthy demand at home keeps a lot of this wine from the international market, so we are delighted to be bringing a slice of it home.

Alongside the wines we serve a small selection of cocktails, as well as Turkish classics—*rakı, çay,* and Turkish coffee—recipes and serving suggestions for which you will find in the drinks chapter.

Although our recipes will, of course, work with more international pairings, serving the Oklava brunch with a Turkish Bloody Mary, surprising your guests with wine from a region they may never have tried before, or rounding off a delicious meal with a cup of Turkish coffee adds a special touch and really brings the Oklava experience to your home.

TOMATO, RAW ONION, PURSLANE, CRISP BREAD & MINT SALAD

SERVES 2–4

14 oz (400 g) stale bread, torn into ⅛ in (3 cm) chunks (old Baharat bread would be perfect; see page 46)

½ cup (120 ml) best-quality extra-virgin olive oil

7 oz (200 g,) tomatoes, best you can find, in different shapes and sizes

1 onion, thinly sliced

1 large bunch of purslane, leaves whole and stalks thinly sliced

4 long green Turkish peppers (Charleston peppers; use ordinary peppers if you can't find them), sliced

1 large handful mint leaves, shredded

1 handful flat leaf parsley

2 tablespoons red wine vinegar, or any good-quality vinegar

flaky sea salt and freshly ground black pepper

This salad is a version of one my *nene* makes. Hers is just a salad of yummy things from her garden, dressed with homemade olive oil and Turkish red wine vinegar. I very fondly remember eating this alongside the little fried fish she used to make; I would soak up the juices from the salad bowl with her freshly baked bread. Here I have combined all of that by putting the crisp bread into the salad to soak up the juices. Purslane grows wild throughout North America, and you can look for it in farmers' markets. If you can't find it, watercress or baby spinach make good substitutes. This salad is great served alongside Fried Red Mullet, Pickled Apricots & Caper Leaves (see page 123).

Preheat the oven to 325°F (160°C). Put the stale bread on a baking tray and coat with 2 tablespoons of the olive oil and a little salt. Bake for about 15 minutes, or until crisp, checking it occasionally.

———

Cut the tomatoes into bite-sized pieces and place in a large bowl with the onion, purslane, peppers, mint, and parsley. Once the crisp bread has cooled, add that too.

———

Season with salt and pepper and add the remaining olive oil and the vinegar. (You can adjust the oil and vinegar quantities depending on how much dressing you like.)

TOMATO-POMEGRANATE SALAD WITH PARSLEY

This is a version of *gavurdağ salatasi*, a famous salad from Turkey that also includes walnuts. It's inspired by a restaurant in Istanbul called Zubeyir, which turns out some of the best kebabs known to man. On my first visit I was encouraged by the waiter to order this salad, so I did—and it was utterly delicious. It's important to chop the vegetables very small so that they mingle with one another, but they don't have to be perfect cubes. This salad is fantastic served with fatty meats.

Mix all the ingredients together in a large bowl and season with salt. It is best to let the salad sit for 5 minutes before serving. If you prefer, you can add more pomegranate molasses, depending on how acidic you like it.

SERVES 2–4

3 plum tomatoes, finely chopped

2 long green Turkish peppers (Charleston peppers; use ordinary peppers if you can't find them), finely chopped

1 large bunch of flat leaf parsley, finely chopped

1 red onion, finely chopped

3½ tablespoons pomegranate molasses

3½ tablespoons extra-virgin olive oil

flaky sea salt

ROMAINE LETTUCE SALAD WITH CANDIED WALNUTS & FETA DRESSING

I have been developing this recipe for quite a few years now. The idea initially came to me when I had an amazing salad at a fish restaurant called Uskumru in Istanbul. A bowl full of wonderful greens came to the table with a cheesy dressing. I couldn't work out exactly what was in it, so in my very broken Turkish (some days I speak it better than others) I asked the waiter. The answer was 14 ingredients, and he wouldn't tell me any of them! This salad is pretty different from the one I got served that day. The best place to find candied walnuts is in a Turkish supermarket; they look like little black golf balls in syrup. They are candied when still in their green shells, fresh from the tree.

Start by making the dressing: place all the ingredients in a blender and process until smooth.

—

Slice the walnuts into ⅛ in (3 mm) slices. Lay all the lettuce leaves out on a tray with their cupped sides facing up. Spread the feta dressing inside all the leaves. Dot the walnut slices across the lettuce, then sprinkle on the chives. Finally, using a fine grater, grate the pecorino all across the top. Transfer to plates and serve.

SERVES 4

4 candied walnuts in syrup, or 1 cup (3½ oz/100 g) walnuts, toasted

1 head of Romaine lettuce, separated into leaves

small bunch of chives, thinly sliced

1 oz (30 g) pecorino or hard sheep's cheese

FOR THE DRESSING

10½ oz (300 g) Turkish white cheese or feta

1 garlic clove

1 teaspoon dried oregano

1 tablespoon honey

freshly squeezed juice of 1 lemon

scant ½ cup (100 ml) extra-virgin olive oil

⅓ cup (80 ml) water

SALAD OF GREEN BEANS, CUCUMBER, FENNEL & KALE WITH A TOMATO DRESSING

SERVES 4

1 fennel bulb

½ cucumber, cut into 2 in (5 cm) batons

2½ cups (1¾ oz/50 g) arugula

1 handful mint leaves, shredded

FOR THE KALE

9 oz (250 g) kale, central stalks sliced out and the leaves torn into small pieces

1 tablespoon extra-virgin olive oil

FOR THE BEANS

⅔ cup (150 ml) extra-virgin olive oil

1 onion, thinly sliced

4 garlic cloves, thinly sliced

1 teaspoon tomato purée

9 oz (250 g) Romano beans, trimmed and sliced diagonally into ¼ in (5 mm) strips

4 tomatoes, coarsely grated

2 tablespoons sherry vinegar

flaky sea salt and freshly ground black pepper

The Turks love all kinds of beans, fresh or dried. Generally, they are cooked or dressed in lots of olive oil and tomato and served either as a vegetarian dish or cooked with lamb. Here I have made the dish into more of a salad, which is great for lunch or a light dinner. Find the best-quality beans you can in season— when they're at their best they have an incredible sweet flavor.

First prepare the beans. Preheat the oven to 250°F (130°C). In a large, wide saucepan, heat the olive oil over medium heat. Add the onion and stir to coat in the oil. Cover and cook gently for 5–10 minutes, stirring occasionally, until the onion is soft and translucent.

———

Add the garlic and tomato purée and cook for another 5 minutes. Stir in the beans, then cover and cook for another 10 minutes. Now add the tomatoes and season with salt and pepper. Cover and turn the heat right down. Cook for about 30 minutes, stirring occasionally, until the beans are completely soft and tender.

———

Meanwhile, coat the kale leaves in 1 tablespoon olive oil and a little salt. Spread them out flat on a baking tray and bake for about 15 minutes, or until crispy. Check the kale every 5 minutes and move it around on the tray so that it bakes evenly.

———

Check the beans: there should be just enough sauce to coat them. If there is too much, remove the lid and cook to reduce it. Turn the heat off and add the sherry vinegar. Taste and season with salt and pepper as needed. Allow to cool to room temperature before serving.

———

Cut the fennel into quarters lengthways through the root. Discard the dark green parts and cut out the core. Using a mandoline, slice the fennel quarters as paper-thin as you can and place them in ice-cold water for 10 minutes. Alternatively, do this with a knife, but take your time to slice it as thinly as possible. Drain the fennel and dry it.

———

To assemble the salad, put the beans with all the tomato dressing in a large bowl, add the cucumber, fennel, arugula, and mint and season with salt and pepper. Give it all a really good mix. Transfer to a serving dish, scatter with the kale chips, and serve immediately.

FRIED VEGETABLES WITH GARLIC YOGURT & POMEGRANATE

SERVES 4

2 zucchinis, cut lengthways into ¾ in (2 cm) slices

2 eggplants, cut lengthways into ½ in (1 cm) slices

1 teaspoon fine salt

¾–1¼ cups (175–300 ml) extra-virgin olive oil

8 long green Turkish peppers (Charleston peppers; use ordinary peppers if you can't find them), halved lengthways

4 hot Turkish peppers (sivri biber; use any hot chilies if you can't find them), halved lengthways (optional)

2 tablespoons pomegranate molasses

seeds from 1 pomegranate

flaky sea salt and freshly ground black pepper

FOR THE DRESSING

1 cup (250 ml) Turkish or Greek yogurt

½ cup (120 ml) extra-virgin olive oil

1–3 garlic cloves (as much as you like!), finely grated

1 handful mint leaves, shredded

1 handful flat leaf parsley, shredded

Please note, you will be pretty garlicky after eating this! But you will also be licking your lips for more. Frying vegetables like this is pretty common in Turkey and Cyprus, especially during the summer. Find the best-tasting vegetables you can; they are the stars of the show.

Sprinkle the zucchinis and eggplants with the fine salt, put them in a colander, then set aside for 1 hour. This is to remove some of the excess moisture. Meanwhile, whisk together all the ingredients for the dressing with 3 tablespoons water and season with salt and pepper.

——

Rinse the salt off the zucchinis and eggplants, then pat dry with paper towels.

——

In a large, shallow, wide-based pan, heat a quarter of the olive oil. Fry the zucchinis, eggplants, and peppers in batches until golden brown on both sides and cooked through, adding more olive oil as needed. As the vegetables cook, transfer them to a colander to cool, and drain off the excess oil.

——

Once all the vegetables are at room temperature, coat them in the yogurt dressing and season with salt and pepper. Transfer to a serving dish, drizzle over the pomegranate molasses, and scatter with the pomegranate seeds.

ZUCCHINI, FETA & MINT FRITTERS

In Turkey these fritters are known as *mücver*. Traditionally, they also include dill. Now, I know I have Turkish blood and all that, but I really don't like dill. That is why it's not in my recipe, but you can include it if you wish, along with any other herbs or greens you like. You could even try using different cheeses. I first put these on the menu at Trip Kitchen, and I can't say I really thought they would turn out to be as popular as they are, but everyone loves them and we get through loads of them every day. The secret is to add just enough flour so that they hold together when frying. The flour measurement below is not exact—it all depends on how much moisture is in your mixture.

SERVES 4–6

1 teaspoon fine salt

8 zucchinis, coarsely grated

2 bunches of scallions, thinly sliced

1 large bunch of mint, leaves picked and shredded, plus more to serve

1 large egg

1 lb 12 oz (800 g) Turkish white cheese or feta, crumbled

1⅔ cups (7 oz/200 g) all-purpose flour

sunflower oil, for frying

freshly ground black pepper

plain yogurt, to serve

Mix the fine salt and zucchinis together and put them in a colander set over a bowl. Sit a plate directly on top of the zucchinis, then put several weights on top of the plate. Set aside for up to 1 hour to drain.

———

Put the zucchinis in a clean dish towel and roll them up into a tube, twisting the ends like a candy wrapper. Squeeze out as much liquid as you possibly can. Put them into a bowl and add the scallions, mint, egg, cheese, flour, and black pepper. Using your hands, mix together the whole bunch, squeezing it as you go. It is important to combine the ingredients really well, but try to keep a little of the texture of the cheese.

———

Heat the sunflower oil in a deep-fryer to 350°F (180°C). Alternatively, place a deep frying pan over high heat and add enough sunflower oil to cover the fritters. When hot enough, a small cube of bread added to the oil should sizzle immediately. Working in batches of 6–8, shape the fritter mixture into very tight quenelles using 2 identical spoons, and lower them into the oil one at a time. Fry for about 1–2 minutes, or until golden brown and crisp on each side. Remove and drain on paper towels. Repeat with the remaining mixture. The fritters are best served with a little yogurt and extra shredded mint.

FETA, GARLIC &
POPPYSEED CRISPS

These are essentially fancy cheese crackers. But they're incredibly tasty, perfect as snacks or to serve alongside a cheese board. You could even top them with Muhammara (see page 190) and serve them as an hors d'œuvre.

MAKES 18–24 CRISPS

7 oz (200 g) Turkish white cheese or feta, finely crumbled

¼ cup (1½ oz/40 g) poppyseeds or nigella seeds

2 garlic cloves, finely grated

3 tablespoons (1½ oz/40 g) unsalted butter, melted

4 sheets of filo pastry, each about 18 x 11 in (47 x 29 cm)

Preheat the oven to 400°F (200°C). Line a large baking tray with parchment paper—the tray needs to be big enough to allow the filo sheets to sit completely flat.

———

Mix the feta, poppyseeds, and grated garlic together. Brush the parchment paper with a little melted butter and lay a sheet of filo on top. Brush the top of the filo with more butter. Distribute one third of the feta mixture across the filo in a thin, even layer. Place another sheet of filo on top, pressing down firmly. Brush the top with butter. Now distribute another third of the feta mixture across the filo in an even layer. Repeat the layering and brushing, finishing with a sheet of filo on top. Place a sheet of parchment paper on the filo and an identical baking tray on top of that. Push down firmly. Remove the top baking tray and paper and cut the filo sandwich into whatever shapes you wish. I like to cut rectangles.

———

Put the sheet of parchment paper back on top, followed by the baking tray. Bake for about 15 minutes, checking halfway through, or until golden brown and crisp. Remove the top baking tray and paper and allow the crisps to cool completely.

CIRCASSIAN CHICKEN

SERVES 10–12 AS PART OF A MEZZE SELECTION

1 whole free-range chicken (about 2¼–3 lb/1–1.3 kg)

4 sprigs of thyme

1 head of garlic, cut in half lengthways

fine salt

2 tablespoons olive oil

1 onion, chopped

1 tablespoon chopped rosemary

4 garlic cloves, finely grated

3 slices white bread, crusts removed and cubed

5 cups (1 lb 2 oz/500 g) walnuts, toasted and crushed

freshly squeezed juice of 1–2 lemons

1–2 tablespoons sweet smoked paprika

small bunch of flat leaf parsley, finely chopped

small bunch of chives, thinly sliced

flaky sea salt and freshly ground black pepper

While I was waiting for Oklava to open, I did a bit of private catering work. Whenever a customer wanted hors d'oeuvres, I made this recipe and served it on crostini, and it was a real winner. Called *çerkez tavuğu* in Turkish, this dish is also great as part of a mezze spread.

Remove all the skin from the chicken and reserve it. Place the chicken, breast-side down in a large pan, along with the thyme and whole garlic, and just cover with water. Add a little fine salt. Bring to a boil over high heat, then turn the heat right down to a gentle simmer. Cook for 45 minutes, turning the chicken over carefully after 30 minutes. Turn the heat off and leave the chicken in the liquid to cool completely.

——

Preheat the oven to 350°F (180°C). Put the chicken skin on a baking tray and bake for 30 minutes, or until golden brown and crisp. Check it halfway through, at which point carefully drain off the excess fat and turn the skin over. Remove and drain on paper towels. Once cool, chop it finely.

——

Strain the liquid from the chicken, reserving the stock. Remove all the chicken meat from the bones and tear it into small pieces as you go.

——

Heat the olive oil in a small pan over medium heat, add the onion, and cook gently, without allowing them to color, for 10 minutes. Add the rosemary and grated garlic and continue to cook for another 2 minutes. Remove and allow to cool slightly.

——

In a food processor, blend the onion mixture with the bread, half the walnuts, a generous 2 cups (500 ml) of the reserved chicken cooking liquid, the juice of 1 lemon, and 1 tablespoon paprika. Blend to a coarse purée.

——

Mix the purée with the chicken, the rest of the walnuts (reserving a few for garnish), and the parsley. Season with salt and pepper and add more lemon juice and paprika if you wish. Place on a serving dish and scatter over the chives, an extra sprinkling of paprika, a drizzle of olive oil, the reserved walnuts, and the chicken skin.

OKLAVA BRUNCH

For as long I can remember, we always went on vacation to Cyprus or Turkey. There are big age gaps between my two older sisters and me—7 and 15 years—and they stopped wanting to go on vacation with my parents as soon as they were old enough, but I still had to for many years ahead. Not that I'm complaining about being taken on vacation, but it became a lot less fun without my sisters there. However, there were two things that always got me excited: one was spending all day in the pool, the other was breakfast.

If we were staying in a hotel in Turkey, breakfast normally involved an array of breads, pastries, fresh and candied fruits, vegetables, yogurt, egg dishes, *Kayseri pastirma*, *sujuk* sausage, cheeses, and much more. If we were in Cyprus, my *nene* would make me toast from bread she had baked during the week by grilling it over an open flame, then serve it with pats of butter and her homemade strawberry jam, or sometimes her hellim (or halloumi, as this cheese is also known). I wish I could give you a recipe for her jam, but it would involve using the strawberries my grandparents grow. You will just have to take my word for it: it is the best strawberry jam in the world.

Breakfast or brunch, as I am about to explain, is not an everyday event; it's definitely a weekend thing. Midweek breakfast tends to involve just a few of the items listed opposite. At Oklava, we do our best to bring a little of that Turkish magic to the brunch we serve every weekend; we like people to take their time and work their way through the options.

BRUNCH MENU

HOUSE-BAKED BREADS
(SEE PAGES 46 & 52)

**FETA, TULUM, KAŞAR
& HELLIM CHEESES**

MARINATED OLIVES

**TAHINI WITH MULBERRY
MOLASSES**

JAM

CANDIED FRUITS

CLOTTED CREAM

HONEY

**SAVORY & SWEET
BÖREKS (SEE PAGES 55,
57, 58 & 204)**

**TOMATOES, CUCUMBERS
& TURKISH PEPPERS**

SEASONAL FRUITS

KAYSERI PASTIRMA

**MENEMEN
(SEE PAGE 40)**

**FRIED EGGS WITH
CYPRIOT PASTIRMA
(SEE PAGE 34)**

**MEDJOOL DATE BUTTER
(SEE PAGE 186)**

ÇAY (SEE PAGE 166)

CYPRIOT PASTIRMA, BROKEN EGGS, SPICY TOMATO & BREAD SAUCE WITH TOMATO-POMEGRANATE SALSA & YOGURT

Mom would sometimes scramble eggs with *pastirma* as a quick dinner—so simple, yet so satisfying! It was the perfect treat. What we Cypriots call *pastirma* is called *sujuk* in mainland Turkey; although it comes in different forms, essentially it is cured beef flavored with lots of garlic and paprika. You can find Cypriot *pastirma* or *sujuk* in most Turkish supermarkets, or you could use soft cooking chorizo or Merguez sausage instead.

Start by making the spicy tomato sauce. Heat the oil in a small saucepan, add the garlic, red chili, pepper flakes, and hot pepper paste and cook gently. Once completely soft, add the puréed tomatoes and water. Season with salt and pepper and simmer over low heat for at least 30 minutes, stirring occasionally. If you can cook it for 1 hour, all the better; it will intensify in flavor. Finish by adding the thyme, sugar, and vinegar. Set aside and keep warm.

⸺

Combine all the ingredients for the salsa in a bowl and season with salt and pepper.

⸺

Slice each pastirma into about 6 pieces. Heat a large non-stick frying pan over medium heat, add the pastirma, and cook gently until nicely browned; there should be enough oil in the sausage, but if the pan seems a little dry, add a touch of olive oil. Crack in the eggs and use a spatula to scramble them into the pastirma. Season with a little salt. I like to cook the eggs so they are still soft, but you can cook them to your liking.

⸺

To assemble, stir the diced bread into the sauce and divide it between 4 bowls. Spoon the pastirma and eggs on top. Finish by putting a big spoonful of salsa in each bowl (making sure you get plenty of the juices), a dollop of yogurt, a final sprinkling of pepper flakes, and some parsley to garnish. I like to serve this with toasted Turkish bread on the side and pats of butter.

SERVES 4

14 oz (400 g) Cypriot pastirma (cured beef) slices

8 large eggs

7 oz (200 g) Turkish bread or a good white crusty loaf, diced into small pieces

¼ cup (60 ml) Turkish or Greek yogurt

1 tablespoon Aleppo pepper flakes (pul biber)

flat leaf parsley, chopped, to garnish

FOR THE SPICY TOMATO SAUCE

scant ½ cup (100 ml) extra-virgin olive oil

4 garlic cloves, sliced

1 red chili, sliced, seeds left in

1 teaspoon Aleppo pepper flakes (pul biber)

1 teaspoon Turkish hot pepper paste (açi biber salçasi)

generous 2 cups (500 ml) puréed tomatoes

scant ½ cup (100 ml) water

1 teaspoon thyme leaves

1 teaspoon sugar

2 teaspoons sherry or red wine vinegar

flaky sea salt and freshly ground black pepper

FOR THE TOMATO-POMEGRANATE SALSA

2 tomatoes, diced

small bunch of flat leaf parsley, shredded

2 tablespoons pomegranate molasses

¼ cup (60 ml) extra-virgin olive oil

SMOKED BACON & MEDJOOL DATE BUTTER TOASTED SANDWICH

SERVES 2

8 rashers smoked bacon

4 slices crusty white bread or sourdough

4 tablespoons Medjool Date Butter (see page 186)

2 tablespoons (1 oz/25 g) unsalted butter, at room temperature

In my opinion, this sandwich at the very least equals a good old-fashioned bacon sandwich, if not tops it.

Cook the bacon to your liking in a frying pan or under the broiler. Spread all 4 slices of bread with the date butter. Divide the bacon between 2 slices and top with the remaining 2 slices, butter side down. Spread the plain butter on the outside of both sandwiches.

Cook them in a toasted sandwich maker until golden and crisp. Alternatively, heat a frying pan over medium heat, add the sandwiches, cover with a piece of parchment paper, and place a weight on top (this ensures a lovely even color). Cook until golden brown, then serve.

BROWN SHRIMP KAYGANA WITH PRESERVED LEMON HOLLANDAISE, ÇEMEN CRUMBS, CHIVES & SHEEP'S CHEESE

SERVES 4

sunflower oil, for cooking

3½ oz (100 g) peeled brown shrimp

small bunch of chives, sliced

1 cup (3½ oz/100 g) finely grated hard sheep's cheese (such as pecorino)

flaky sea salt and freshly ground black pepper

FOR THE ÇEMEN CRUMBS

1 stick (4 oz/115 g) unsalted butter

1 tablespoon Çemen (see page 199)

2½ cups (9 oz/250 g) dried (preferably panko) breadcrumbs

FOR THE BATTER

2 tablespoons all-purpose flour

6 large eggs

2 tablespoons milk

FOR THE PRESERVED LEMON HOLLANDAISE

1 small preserved lemon (see page 201)

2¼ sticks (9 oz/250 g) unsalted butter

1 large egg, plus 2 large egg yolks

freshly squeezed juice of ½ lemon

fine salt

A *kaygana* is essentially a cross between an omelette and a crêpe. You could add some herbs and scallions to the batter and make a stack of them, or create sweet ones with nuts and syrup. But do try this recipe; I think it's a perfect marriage of flavors. Serve it with a big pile of toasted Turkish bread and plenty of butter.

Preheat the oven to 375°F (190°C) and line a baking tray with parchment paper. First make the çemen crumbs: melt the butter with the çemen. Whisk well and stir in the breadcrumbs, ensuring they all get an even coating of butter and çemen; they should turn orange. Spread over the prepared tray. Bake for about 15 minutes, stirring them halfway through. Remove and leave to cool. Turn the oven down to 225°F (110°C).

———

For the batter, put the flour in a bowl and make a well in the center. In a separate bowl, whisk the eggs and milk together. Add to the flour a little at a time, whisking continuously to form a smooth batter.

———

To make the hollandaise, cut the preserved lemon into quarters. Remove the flesh and squeeze the juice into a heatproof bowl. Dice the skin as finely as you can and set aside. Melt the butter in a pan and set aside to cool slightly. Whisk the egg and egg yolks into the lemon juice. Set the bowl over a pan of barely simmering water and whisk until the mixture leaves a trail that holds its shape when the whisk is lifted. Remove from the heat immediately and keep whisking until the eggs have cooled slightly.

———

Put the bowl on a dish towel or non-slip mat. Whisking continuously with one hand, slowly pour in the melted butter with the other. If your hands get tired, pour in the butter a little at a time and whisk it all in before adding more. Once all the butter is incorporated, add the lemon juice and diced preserved lemon skin. Season with a little salt. Place a piece of plastic wrap or parchment paper directly on top to stop a skin from forming.

———

Heat 1 tablespoon oil over medium heat in a frying pan about 8 in (20 cm) in diameter. Scatter a quarter of the shrimps around the pan, then pour in a quarter of the batter, and season with salt and pepper. Cook until the top is lightly golden and the underside is set. Fold in half to make a semicircle and continue to cook for about 20 seconds, then flip it over and cook for another 20 seconds, until both sides are golden. Transfer to a baking tray and keep warm. Repeat this step to make 3 more. Put them all in the oven to warm up for 2–3 minutes.

———

To serve, put one kaygana in the center of each serving plate, drizzle over some hollandaise, and scatter over the chives, çemen crumbs, and grated cheese.

MENEMEN

I make my *menemen* a little differently from most recipes, although everyone has their own version—you can even add feta, *sujuk*, or *Kayseri pastirma*, if you like. Traditionally, you would just sauté the vegetables quite quickly and then scramble the eggs in; if you find good enough produce, you can make it just like that. I prefer to make a ragout first and get the best I can out of all the flavors. You can make the ragout ahead of time and chill it in the fridge. To cook the dish, simply pour more olive oil into a frying pan, add the ragout to heat up gently, then crack in the eggs and cook as described. Long green Turkish peppers (known as Charleston peppers) and hot green sivri peppers are distinctive flavors in Turkish cooking, and are available in most Turkish supermarkets. If you can't get hold of them, just use ordinary green peppers and green chilies respectively.

Heat the oil in a large frying pan, add the onion and peppers, and cook gently over low heat for about 30 minutes, or until completely soft. Add the tomato paste, hot pepper paste, and tomatoes and cook gently for another 30 minutes. Season with a little salt and pepper at this point. Finish the sauce base by adding the sugar and vinegar.

———

Crack the eggs into the pan and, using a spatula, gently cook them, stirring, to a soft scrambled consistency. Season with salt and pepper and then garnish with parsley. Serve with lots of freshly baked bread.

SERVES 4

⅔ cup (150 ml) extra-virgin olive oil

1 onion, diced

4 long green Turkish peppers (Charleston peppers; use ordinary peppers if you can't find them), sliced

4 hot Turkish peppers (sivri biber; use any hot chilies if you can't find them), sliced

½ teaspoon tomato paste

1 teaspoon Turkish hot pepper paste (açi biber salçasi)

4 plum tomatoes, roughly grated in a food processor or by hand

½ teaspoon sugar

½ teaspoon sherry or red wine vinegar

8 large eggs

flat leaf parsley, chopped, to garnish

flaky sea salt and freshly ground black pepper

PISTACHIO-CRUSTED BANANA & TAHINI FRENCH TOAST WITH ORANGE BLOSSOM SYRUP & SMOKED BACON

I first came across stuffed French toast when I started working at The Providores. The restaurant's famous version is stuffed with banana and pecans and served with bacon and verjus syrup. I created this version one day when I needed to use up a pile of small baguettes that had gone stale, so feel free to try it with a baguette too—it will just need longer soaking.

Preheat the oven to 375°F (190°C). Whisk the eggs and cream together in a shallow bowl and set aside. Put the pistachios on a baking tray and bake for about 6 minutes, or until lightly toasted and smelling nutty. Leave them to cool, then crush to a coarse powder in a food processor or with a mortar and pestle, and spread them out on a plate.

———

Peel and roughly crush the bananas in a bowl. Using a spatula, mix the tahini and mascarpone together in a separate bowl, then mix it through the bananas. Spread this mixture over 2 slices of bread. Top with the remaining slices and press down gently to stick the whole sandwich together.

———

Dip the sandwiches in the egg and cream mixture, turning to coat well, then leave them to soak up the mixture for 10 minutes, turning halfway through to make sure both sides get soaked.

———

Set a large frying pan over medium heat and add the oil and butter. Once the butter has melted, add the sandwiches and cook for about 5 minutes on each side until golden brown.

———

Meanwhile, in another frying pan or under the broiler, cook the bacon to your liking (for me it has to be crispy!).

———

Remove the sandwiches from the pan and put them on a baking tray. Brush each side with some orange blossom syrup, then dip them straight into the pistachio crumbs, coating well on both sides. Cut in half and serve topped with the bacon and more syrup.

SERVES 2

2 large eggs

scant 1 cup (200 ml) heavy cream

1¼ cups (5½ oz/150 g) peeled pistachios

1 large or 2 small bananas

2 tablespoons tahini

3 heaped tablespoons mascarpone

4 slices crusty white bread

1 tablespoon sunflower oil

2 tablespoons (1 oz/25 g) unsalted butter

6 rashers smoked bacon

½ quantity Orange Blossom Syrup (see page 200)

SAVORY
BAKES

BAHARAT-SPICED BREAD

This recipe is adapted slightly from the village bread my *nene* makes. I have fond memories of eating it fresh from the clay oven with pats of butter. She perfumes the bread with just a little *baharat*, which she mixes in after the dough has proofed once, so that it ripples throughout the bread. *Baharat* is a blend of spices that usually includes allspice, cloves, cinnamon, and nutmeg, although everyone has their own recipe, which sometimes includes other spices. My *nene* would also break some of the bread into chunks as soon as it was baked, then dry them out in the residual heat of the oven. This is known as *peksimet*, or dried bread, and is usually doused in water just before serving.

If using fresh yeast, dissolve it in about ⅔ cup (150 ml) lukewarm water with the sugar, then mix the flour and salt in a large bowl, make a well in the center, and add the frothy yeast mixture along with the olive oil and baharat. If using dried yeast, mix it with the flour, sugar, and salt in a large bowl. Make a well in the center and add the olive oil, baharat, and ⅔ cup (150 ml) lukewarm water.

——

Using your hands, begin to incorporate the flour into the liquid. Slowly add more lukewarm water, a little at a time, mixing with your hands to form a dough. (You'll probably need around another ⅔ cup/ 150 ml, but don't add it all at once; you'll only need extra if it feels dry). Tip the dough onto a lightly floured surface. Knead for about 5 minutes, or until smooth.

——

Put the dough in a clean bowl and cover it with a clean, damp dish towel. Place somewhere slightly warm to speed up the rising process; the dough should double in size, within 45–60 minutes.

——

Preheat the oven to 475°F (240°C). Punch the dough down in the bowl, then tip it onto a very lightly floured surface. Knead the dough for around 30 seconds. Roll the bread into a cylinder about 3 in (8 cm) in diameter. Cut it into 3 equal pieces, then push them together lightly. Place the sesame seeds on a large plate. Brush the dough all over with a little water and press it lightly into the sesame seeds, turning so it is covered on all sides. Place on a lightly floured nonstick baking tray and set aside to proof. It should double in size within about 45 minutes.

——

Half-fill a glass with cold water. Put the dough in the oven, tip the water directly onto the bottom of your oven, and immediately close the door. Bake for 20 minutes, then lower the heat to 400°F (200°C) and continue to bake for another 10–20 minutes, or until golden brown. To check if it is cooked, tap on the bottom and listen for a hollow sound. If it doesn't sound hollow, return it to the oven for a little longer. Remove and leave to cool down considerably before cutting it.

MAKES 1 LOAF

½ oz (15 g) fresh yeast or 1 x ¼ oz (7 g) envelope instant yeast

½ teaspoon sugar

3¼ cups (1 lb/450 g) bread flour, plus more for dusting

1 teaspoon fine salt

1 teaspoon olive oil

1 tablespoon baharat (see page 193; also available in Turkish supermarkets)

3 tablespoons mixed white and black sesame seeds

PILAVUNA

MAKES 12

about 1 lb 10 oz (750 g) hellim (or halloumi) cheese, finely grated

1 tablespoon dried mint

1 teaspoon baking powder

2 heaped tablespoons fine semolina

¾ cup (3½ oz/100 g) raisins (optional)

4–6 large eggs

FOR THE DOUGH

6 cups (1 lb 10 oz/750 g) all-purpose flour

1 teaspoon fine salt

1 x ¼ oz (7 g) envelope instant yeast

about 2 cups (450 ml) lukewarm water

1 teaspoon sugar

1 teaspoon olive oil

TO FINISH

¾ cup (3½ oz/100 g) sesame seeds, moistened with 1 tablespoon water (optional)

1–2 large eggs, lightly beaten

Pilavuna **are very traditional Cypriot pastries, perfect as a teatime treat or for breakfast. My mom and her friends often gather some evenings to whip up a massive batch of these, along with other pastries. They have a coffee and gossip, and then each person takes home their share of baked goods.**

First make the dough: put the flour in a large bowl and add the salt on one side and the yeast and the sugar on the other. Gradually add the water, incorporating the flour with your hands as you go. Once a dough has formed, turn it onto a clean work surface and knead until smooth. Clean any crumbs out of the bowl, grease it with the olive oil, then add the dough. Cover it with plastic wrap or a damp cloth and leave to proof in a warm place until doubled in size (about 45 minutes).

———

Meanwhile, make the filling. Put the hellim in a bowl with the mint, baking powder, semolina, and raisins, if using, and mix well. Work in the eggs one at a time until a dough forms. You might need a little extra semolina to achieve this. Divide the mixture into 12 equal pieces. Preheat the oven to 425°F (220°C). Line 2–3 baking trays (depending on size) with parchment paper.

———

Turn the dough onto a lightly floured work surface and knead lightly for a minute or so. Roll it into a large sausage shape, then divide it into 12 equal pieces. Roll each piece of dough into a 4 x 3 in (10 x 8 cm) rectangle, about ¹/₈ in (3 mm) thick. Press one side of the dough into the moistened sesame seeds so that they stick to it. Return it to the work surface and place 1 portion of the filling in the center. Fold up the edges of the dough to make a rectangular shape, leaving some of the filling exposed in the center. Place on the baking sheet and repeat the process for the remaining filling and dough.

———

Brush the top of the pastries with beaten egg to glaze and sprinkle over a few extra sesame seeds if you wish. Bake for 20–25 minutes, or until golden brown all over.

BLACK OLIVE, HELLIM, ONION & MINT LOAF

This is one of my favorites of my Mom's recipes. It features quite a bit of olive oil, which gives a lovely, almost focaccia-like texture—perfect with a cup of tea in the afternoon. Make sure you use the best olives you can find, as these are key to the flavor.

In a large bowl, mix together the flour, yeast, salt, and sugar. Add the water and olive oil to form a thick batter. Add the remaining ingredients and mix well.

Oil a roasting pan measuring about 14 x 10 x 2 in (36 x 26 x 5 cm) or a round baking pan about 12 in (30 cm) in diameter. Place the batter into the pan and even out. Leave to proof until doubled in size.

———

Preheat the oven to 400°F (210°C). Bake for 45–60 minutes or until golden brown. Insert a skewer to check; if it comes out clean, the loaf is ready. Leave to cool.

SERVES 14–16

8 cups (2 lb 4 oz/1 kg) all-purpose flour

2 x ¼ oz (7 g) envelopes instant yeast

1 teaspoon fine salt

1 teaspoon sugar

3⅓ cups (800 ml) water

1 cup (250 ml) extra-virgin olive oil, plus extra for greasing

1 onion, finely chopped

9 oz (250 g) hellim (or halloumi) cheese, cut into ½ in (1 cm) cubes

3¼ cups (1 lb 2 oz/500 g) good-quality pitted black olives, roughly chopped

2 tablespoons dried mint

CHEESE, SCALLION, BAHARAT & GARLIC BÖREKS

MAKES 18–20

1 lb 2 oz (500 g) mixed cheese, grated

1 bunch of scallions, thinly sliced

large bunch of flat leaf parsley, finely shredded

2 tablespoons baharat (see page 193; also available in Turkish supermarkets)

4 garlic cloves, finely grated

1 quantity Pide dough (see page 60)

all-purpose flour, for dusting

2 tablespoons extra virgin olive oil, for drizzling

These are perfect for an afternoon snack or even for breakfast, and the baharat gives a lovely background perfume. Feel free to use whatever kind of cheese you prefer, or even just one type. I like to use a mix of aged kaşar cheese, feta, and hellim (also called halloumi), but mature Cheddar, Parmesan, and soft goat cheese work well too.

Combine the cheeses, scallions, parsley, baharat, and garlic. Divide into 2 equal portions and set aside.

————

Once the pide dough has risen, punch it down and divide into 2 equal balls. Keep one covered and, on a lightly floured work surface, roll the other into a rough circle about $^1/_{16}$ in (2 mm) thick. Place tablespoons of the cheese mixture on one half of the dough, ensuring each spoonful is at least 1¼ in (3 cm) from the next. Fold the other half of the dough over them and press it down quite firmly around the piles of filling.

————

Using either a pizza cutter or a small sharp knife, cut around the piles of filling to make random shapes. If the edges of each börek have not stuck together securely, use a little water to seal them. Place the böreks on a lightly floured surface. Repeat the process with the remaining dough and filling.

————

Heat a large, heavy-based frying pan over medium-high heat. Place 4 or 5 böreks in the dry pan and cook for 2–3 minutes, turning regularly, or until dark brown spots appear. Repeat until all the böreks are cooked. Drizzle with olive oil to serve.

SPICED BEEF & CHEESE SAUCE POĞAÇAS

When in need of a top-up of Turkish ingredients, I often stop by my local TFC (Turkish Food Center). These shops are scattered all around London and have their own in-house bakeries, which make the most incredible baked goods. I find it pretty hard to resist their *poğaças*, which are small, brioche-like buns that are often stuffed with feta and parsley. You can experiment with different types of filling, but don't put anything too wet inside or they might pop open.

Start by making the dough. Combine the flour, yeast, sugar, and salt in a bowl. Make a well in the center and add 2 eggs, the melted butter, yogurt, and water. Bring together with your hands and knead for about 5 minutes on a lightly floured surface to form a smooth dough. Place in a clean bowl and cover with a clean damp dish towel. Set aside to rise for about 45 minutes, or until doubled in size.

Meanwhile, make the filling. Heat the oil in a large saucepan over high heat. Add the ground meat and cook, using a whisk to break it up, until browned all over, stirring occasionally. This will take about 8 minutes. Add the onions and continue to cook over medium heat until lightly browned. Now add the remaining ingredients (except the sesame seeds) and cook over medium-low heat for about 20 minutes. Set aside to cool.

To make the cheese sauce, melt the butter in a medium saucepan. Add the flour, whisk well, and cook over low heat for 5 minutes. Add one-third of the milk and whisk it in until smooth. Repeat with the remaining milk. Continue to cook over low heat, whisking occasionally, for 15 minutes. Finally, add both the cheeses and cook for another 2 minutes. Set aside and allow to cool.

Preheat the oven to 400°F (200°C) and line a large baking tray with parchment paper. Punch down the dough and divide it into 12–14 equal pieces on a lightly floured surface. Roll a piece of dough into a circle about 5 in (12 cm) in diameter. Place a heaped tablespoon of cheese sauce in the center and spread it out slightly, ensuring you leave a ¾ in (2 cm) border all the way around the edge. Do the same with the beef filling. Fold over the dough to make a pasty shape, ensuring you press down the edges to seal them well. Place it on the prepared baking tray. Repeat with the remaining dough, leaving a ¾ in (2 cm) gap between each one (you might need more than one baking tray).

Beat the remaining egg with about 2 tablespoons water, brush the pastries with this mixture, and sprinkle with sesame seeds. Bake for 16–18 minutes, or until golden brown.

MAKES 12

2 tablespoons sunflower oil

1 lb 2 oz (500 g) ground beef

2 onions, finely chopped

large bunch of flat leaf parsley, finely chopped

2 tablespoons Turkish hot pepper paste (açi biber salçasi)

1 heaped tablespoon tomato paste

1 teaspoon ground cumin

1 teaspoon ground fennel

1 teaspoon sweet smoked paprika

1 teaspoon ground coriander

⅓ cup (1¾ oz/50 g) mixed white and black sesame seeds

flaky sea salt and freshly ground black pepper

FOR THE DOUGH

5⅗ cups (1 lb 9 oz/700 g) all-purpose flour

1 x ¼ oz (7 g) envelope instant yeast

3 tablespoons sugar

¾ teaspoon fine salt

3 large eggs

1½ sticks (6 oz/170 g) unsalted butter, melted

1¼ cups (300 ml) Greek or Turkish strained yogurt

scant ½ cup (100 ml) water

FOR THE SAUCE

7 tablespoons (3½ oz/100 g) unsalted butter

generous ½ cup (2¾ oz/75 g) all-purpose flour

3⅓ cups (800 ml) milk

¾ cup (2¾ oz/80 g) grated hard cheese, such as pecorino

1¼ cups (5 oz/140 g) grated hellim (or halloumi) cheese

BAHARAT & CHILI-SPICED FISH BÖREKS

MAKES 10–12

1 egg white, for brushing

12 sheets of filo pastry

sunflower oil, for frying

FOR THE FILLING

scant ½ cup (100 ml) extra-virgin olive oil

1 large onion, diced

3 garlic cloves, finely grated

2 tablespoons sweet red pepper paste (tatli biber salçasi)

1 tablespoon baharat (see page 193; also available in Turkish supermarkets)

2–4 tablespoons Urfa chili flakes (isot biber), depending on how hot you like it

2 teaspoons sweet smoked paprika

10½ oz (300 g) skinless white fish fillet, diced

⅓ cup(1¾ oz/50 g) raisins

1 large handful mint leaves, shredded

1 large handful flat leaf parsley, shredded

flaky sea salt and freshly ground black pepper

These *böreks* would work well with all types of white fish, such as pollock, cod, or haddock. You could even mix some shrimp or crab in there too. I think they're great as party food, or if you want to be a little fancy, you could serve one of them alongside a piece of roasted fish for a dinner party.

Start by making the filling. Heat the oil in a large frying pan, add the onion, and cook gently over medium heat until golden brown. Add the garlic, sweet pepper paste, baharat, chili flakes, and paprika and continue to cook for 5 minutes. Add the fish and raisins and cook for another 5 minutes, or until the fish is just cooked through. Remove from the heat and season with salt and black pepper. Transfer to a tray and spread it out to cool down quickly. Once cool, mix in the herbs and divide the mixture into 12 equal portions.

Beat the egg white lightly in a small bowl, just to break it up. Place a sheet of filo on your work surface with the long side nearest you. Fold it in half from left to right. Now place one portion of the filling in the center of the edge closest to you, leaving a 1½ in (4 cm) gap on each side. From the edge closest to you, fold the filo over the filling twice. Now fold in the sides. Brush the remaining pastry with egg white and continue to roll it up, ensuring you encase the filling tightly. Repeat this process with the remaining filo and filling.

Heat the oil in a deep-fryer to 350°F (180°C). Alternatively, place a deep frying pan over high heat and add enough oil to cover the böreks. When hot enough, a small cube of bread added to the oil should sizzle immediately.

Carefully add 4 böreks to the oil and fry for 1–2 minutes, or until golden brown. You might need to turn them over halfway if they don't color evenly. Remove and drain on paper towels, then fry the remaining böreks in the same way. Serve immediately.

SPINACH & FETA BÖREK

I'm not usually a huge fan of spinach, but in this *börek* I am. You can use other fillings too, such as a selection of cheeses, nuts, mushrooms, and so on. Made as a large pie, rather than individual pastries, this is a favorite at Oklava as part of our brunch.

MAKES 1 X 12 IN
(30 CM) PIE
(8–12 SERVINGS)

Heat 2 tablespoons of the oil in a small saucepan, add the onions, and cook gently until golden brown. Place a large heavy-based pan over high heat with one-third of the remaining olive oil. Add one-third of the spinach and cook until just wilted. Transfer to a colander set over a bowl and repeat the process with the rest of the spinach and oil in 2 batches. Squeeze out as much water from the spinach as possible, then combine it with the cooked onions and season with salt and pepper. Whisk together the eggs and cream.

———

Preheat the oven to 400°F (210°C). Crumble the cheese into a bowl and stir in the oregano and parsley. To assemble the börek, start by brushing a 12 x 8 x 1½ in (30 x 20 x 4 cm) baking tray or a 12 in (30 cm) round baking pan with butter. Lay a sheet of filo in the tray, allowing it to hang over the edges, brush the filo with butter, then add another sheet on top. Repeat the process with 4 more filo layers, making sure some pastry hangs over on all sides.

———

Spread half the spinach mixture over the filo and pour in one-quarter of the egg mixture. Layer up another 4 sheets of filo, this time cutting each sheet in half so that the pastry does not hang over the edges, and brushing with butter in between each one. Now spread half the cheese mixture over the top and pour in one-quarter of the egg mixture. Top with another 4 halved sheets of filo, brushing each one with butter as before.

———

Spread over the remaining spinach mixture and pour in one-quarter of the egg mixture. Top with another 4 halved sheets of filo, brushing them with butter as before. Now spread over the final layer of cheese mixture, pour in the remaining egg mixture, and press the whole thing down evenly.

———

Fold the overhanging edges of filo over the top. Finish the börek with 6 whole sheets of filo, brushing with butter in between each one, and pushing in the edges with the handle of a metal spoon as you go. Brush the top with butter. Bake for 25 minutes, then turn the oven down to 375°F (190°C) and bake for another 20 minutes. Allow the börek to cool before cutting it into 12 portions.

- scant ½ cup (100 ml) extra-virgin olive oil
- 2 onions, finely chopped
- 2 lb 4 oz (1 kg) large leaf spinach with stalks, roughly chopped (or 2 large bags of spinach leaves, 1 lb/450 g each)
- 2 large eggs
- scant 1 cup (200 ml) heavy cream
- 1 lb 12 oz (800 g) Turkish white cheese or feta
- 1 tablespoon dried oregano
- large bunch of flat leaf parsley, finely chopped
- 1 stick (4 oz/115 g) unsalted butter, melted
- 24 sheets of filo pastry, about 19 x 10 in (48 x 25 cm) each
- flaky sea salt and freshly ground black pepper

PIDES

When designing Oklava, there were two features I just had to include. One is our barbecue and the other is our big stone oven, where we make our *pides* and *lahmacun*, Turkish versions of pizza. The heat is so intense that you get an amazing crust on breads and pastry products. Chances are you won't have a stone oven at home, but these *pides* work really well in a conventional oven too. *Lahmacuns* don't, however, which is why I haven't included a recipe here. Traditionally, *pides* have toppings such as Turkish cheeses, peppers, onions, tomatoes, diced lamb, or chicken. One of my favorites, which I always asked for when I was younger, has a little tomato sauce, Cypriot *pastirma,* and an egg, and is delicious served hot or cold. As with everything we do at Oklava, these traditional *pides* are our source of inspiration for creating more contemporary versions. You could give this simple version a try before moving on to our more complex ones. For example, try mixing ground lamb with diced onions, peppers, tomato, and parsley, then place the raw mixture on rolled-out pide dough and bake as below. Alternatively, you could try a mix of mozzarella, Cheddar, crumbly goat cheese, and chopped parsley.

PIDE DOUGH

If using fresh yeast, dissolve it in a little water. Place the flour, yeast, olive oil, salt, and sugar in a large bowl or stand mixer. Mix well, then slowly begin to add the water, mixing with one hand. Do not add all the water at once, since you might not need it all. Add just enough to form a dough that doesn't stick to your hands too much.

———

Tip it onto a clean, lightly floured surface. Knead for 5 minutes, or until a smooth dough forms. Shape it into a ball, put it in a clean bowl, and cover with a clean damp dish towel. Leave it somewhere warm for 45–60 minutes until doubled in size.

———

Once the dough has risen, punch it back in the bowl, then tip onto a lightly floured surface. Roll the dough into a long sausage, then divide it into 6 equal pieces. Roll each piece into a ball, put them on a lightly floured surface, and cover with a damp dish towel until you're ready to use them.

———

Preheat the oven to 475°F (240°C). Put a pizza stone or a large flat baking tray in the oven.

———

To make the pides (I suggest making them one at a time), place a ball of dough on a floured work surface and roll into an oval about 16 x 6 in (40 x 15 cm). Combine the raw ingredients of your chosen filling, place them on the rolled-out dough, and fold in the edges as shown opposite. Slide your pide onto a very flat baking sheet, then place this on the preheated tray or stone and bake for 10–12 minutes. Make 5 more in the same way. If you want to serve them all together, reheat in the oven before serving.

generous 4½ cups (1 lb 6 oz/ 625 g) white bread flour (we use a Turkish flour called Bodrum), plus extra for dusting

⅓ oz (12 g) fresh yeast or 1 x ¼ oz (7 g) envelope instant yeast

1 tablespoon extra-virgin olive oil

1 teaspoon fine salt

1 teaspoon sugar

about 1½ cups (350 ml) lukewarm water, plus 1 or 2 tablespoons more, if needed

SIMPLE FILLING 1

1 lb 2 oz (500 g) ground lamb

1 onion, diced

2 peppers, chopped

4 tomatoes, chopped

small bunch of parsley, chopped

SIMPLE FILLING 2

1¾ cups (7 oz/200 g) grated Cheddar cheese

1¾ cups (7 oz/200 g) diced mozzarella cheese

7 oz (200 g) goat cheese, crumbled

small bunch of parsley, chopped

CHICKEN & GARLIC KÖFTE PIDE WITH CHILI YOGURT, SMOKED SALSA, WALNUTS & FETA

MAKES 6

1 quantity Pide dough (see page 60)

flour, for dusting

2 tablespoons (1 oz/25 g) unsalted butter, melted

½ quantity Fried Dried Chili Yogurt (see page 199)

1¼ cups (4¼ oz/120 g) walnuts, lightly toasted and crushed

4¼ oz (120 g) feta

small handful mint, finely shredded

small handful flat leaf parsley, finely shredded

flaky sea salt

FOR THE CHICKEN KÖFTE

1 lb 2 oz (500 g) ground chicken

1 red pepper, finely diced

1 onion, finely diced

3 garlic cloves, finely grated

6 tablespoons sweet pepper paste (tatlı biber salçası)

small bunch of flat leaf parsley, finely chopped

fine salt

FOR THE SALSA

6 banana shallots, skin on, halved lengthways

9 oz (250 g) baby plum tomatoes

10 long green Turkish peppers (Charleston peppers; use ordinary peppers if you can't find them)

2 tablespoons pomegranate molasses

1 teaspoon sweet smoked paprika

1 teaspoon dried oregano

scant ½ cup (100 ml) extra-virgin olive oil

Here is one of those recipes that just came to me, this time during a conversation with my sous chef, Nick. He was telling me that he missed cooking the lamb *köfte* we'd once had on the menu, while I was thinking that I wanted to put a new meat *pide* on. The result was that I combined them.

Preheat the oven to 475°F (240°C). Put a pizza stone or a large flat baking tray in the oven.

———

Mix together all the ingredients for the chicken köfte. Season with salt, then fry a little and taste it: adjust the seasoning, as necessary, and divide the mixture into 6 equal portions.

———

To make the smoked salsa, you'll need a hot barbecue or a very hot ridged grill pan. Working in batches, cook the shallots, tomatoes, and peppers until their skins are blackened. Allow them to become cool enough to handle, then peel off the shallot and pepper skins and dice the flesh. Peel and crush the tomatoes with the back of a fork and combine them in a bowl with the shallots and peppers and the remaining ingredients for the salsa. Season with salt.

———

Opposite: *Chicken & Garlic Köfte Pide with Chili Yogurt, Smoked Salsa, Walnuts & Feta (top); Braised Octopus Pide with Ricotta, Green Olives, Honey, Pickled Caper Shoots & Thyme (center), and Cheese Sauce Pide with Charred Leeks & Crispy Potatoes (bottom).*

To make the pides (I suggest making them one at a time), roll out a ball of dough on a floured surface into a large oval shape about 16 x 6 in (40 x 15 cm). Spread one portion of the chicken köfte mixture down the center, leaving a border of 1¼ in (3 cm) around the edge. Season with a little flaky salt. Fold in the sides as shown on page 61, and pinch the ends together really well so that the pide doesn't unravel during baking.

———

Slide your pide onto a very flat baking sheet, then place it on the preheated baking tray or pizza stone. Bake for 10–12 minutes, or until golden brown and crisp on the outside. Remove and brush the sides of the pide with the melted butter, then top with some smoked salsa, chili yogurt, walnuts, feta, mint, and parsley. Make 5 more in the same way. If you want to serve the pides all together, set them aside after baking, then reheat and garnish as described.

BRAISED OCTOPUS PIDE WITH RICOTTA, GREEN OLIVES, HONEY, PICKLED CAPER SHOOTS & THYME

The flavors of this *pide*—my favorite—are quite unusual and I find that customers often love it because they aren't expecting it to work. If you're not a fan of sweet with savory I suggest leaving out the honey. Use capers if you can't find pickled caper shoots (they are available in Turkish supermarkets) and substitute pre-marinated octopus if you can't source fresh.

MAKES 6

3 lb 5 oz–4 lb 8 oz (1.5-2 kg) octopus

⅔ cup (150 ml) extra-virgin olive oil

1 lemon, halved

2 sprigs of rosemary

3 garlic cloves, lightly crushed

3 tablespoons Turkish red wine vinegar, or any good-quality vinegar

1 quantity Pide dough (see page 60)

flour, for dusting

6 heaped tablespoons ricotta cheese

3 tablespoons thyme leaves

scant ½ cup (4¼ oz/120 g) good-quality green olives, pitted

2 tablespoons (1 oz/25 g) unsalted butter, melted

½ cup (2¾ oz/80 g) pickled caper shoots, or capers

6 tablespoons honey

½ cup (1¾ oz/50 g) shaved ricotta salata cheese (or use Parmesan), to garnish

flaky sea salt and freshly ground black pepper

Preheat the oven to 325°F (160°C). Put the octopus in a large roasting pan along with half the olive oil and a lemon half. Cover with foil and bake for 1½–2 hours until tender. The best way to check if the octopus is ready is to cut a little off and taste it; if it is chewy, it needs a little longer. Remove and drain the octopus and allow it to cool completely.

———

If you happen to be having a barbecue, grill the octopus over hot coals until well colored and a little charred on both sides. Alternatively, heat a ridged griddle pan until very hot and cook the octopus in the same way.

———

Preheat the oven to 475°F (240°C). Put a pizza stone or a large flat baking tray in the oven. Cut off the octopus legs and cut them into ½ in (1 cm) slices. Remove the beak and any other tough bits in the center, then rinse the head and cut it into ½ in (1 cm) slices.

———

Put the remaining olive oil in a bowl along with the rosemary, garlic, and vinegar, and season with salt and pepper. Leave the octopus to marinate in the refrigerator for as long as you can, preferably overnight.

———

To make the pides (I suggest making them one at a time), roll out a ball of dough on a floured surface into a large oval shape about 16 x 6 in (40 x 15 cm). Spread one heaped tablespoon of the ricotta down the middle, leaving a 1¼ in (3 cm) border around the edge. Sprinkle with some thyme and green olives and season with salt and pepper. Top with a layer of the octopus. Fold in the sides as shown on page 61, and pinch the ends together really well so that the pide doesn't unravel during baking.

———

Slide your pide onto a very flat baking sheet, then place it on the preheated baking tray or pizza stone. Bake for about 10–12 minutes, or until golden brown and crisp on the outside. Remove and brush the sides with the melted butter, then top with the caper shoots, a drizzle of honey, and some ricotta shavings. Make 5 more in the same way. If you want to serve the pides all together, set them aside after baking, then reheat and garnish as described.

CHEESE SAUCE PIDE WITH CHARRED LEEKS & CRISPY POTATOES

MAKES 6

6 large leeks, dark green parts removed

3 large potatoes

sunflower oil, for frying

fine salt

1 quantity Pide dough (see page 60)

flour, for dusting

2 tablespoons dried oregano

2 tablespoons sesame seeds, lightly toasted

2 tablespoons (1 oz/25 g) unsalted butter, melted

6 tablespoons tulum cheese (or use feta or a crumbly goat cheese)

flaky sea salt

FOR THE CHEESE SAUCE

5 tablespoons (2½ oz/65 g) unsalted butter

⅓ cup (1¾ oz/45 g) all-purpose flour

generous 2 cups (500 ml) milk

½ cup (1¾ oz/50 g) grated pecorino cheese (or any hard cheese)

¾ cup (2¾ oz/80 g) grated hellim (or halloumi) cheese

This *pide* is very subtle in its flavors. The cheese sauce is not too strong and provides a lovely creamy center. You could also drizzle a little garlic oil over the leeks for an extra layer of flavor. Tulum is generally sold in jars and has a very strong, almost Parmesan-like flavor.

Preheat the oven to 475°F (240°C). Put a pizza stone or a large flat baking tray in the oven.

First make the cheese sauce: melt the butter in a saucepan over medium heat, then whisk in the flour. Add one-third of the milk and whisk until smooth. Add the remaining milk in 2 batches, whisking well each time. Turn the heat right down and cook gently for about 15 minutes, whisking occasionally. Finally, whisk in the cheese—the pecorino will melt, but the hellim won't. Transfer to a shallow tray and allow to cool completely.

Put the leeks on a baking tray and roast for about 20 minutes, turning halfway through, until the outside is charred. For a smoky flavor, the barbecue is the best place to cook them. Peel off the burned outer layer of the leeks, leaving on a few of the charred bits, as they provide good flavor. Cut the leeks into ¾ in (2 cm) slices.

Slice the potatoes as finely as possible on a mandoline (watch your fingers!). Place in a bowl of warm water to remove excess

starch, then lay them out to dry on a clean dish towel. Heat the oil in a deep-fryer to 325°F (160°C). Alternatively, heat a ¾ in (2 cm) depth of oil in a deep frying pan over high heat. When hot enough, a small cube of bread added to the oil should sizzle immediately. Put a batch of potatoes in the fryer, one at a time to avoid them sticking together, and fry until golden and crisp. Remove and drain on paper towels, then season with fine salt. Repeat with the remaining potatoes.

To make the pides (I suggest making them one at a time), roll out a ball of dough on a floured surface into a large oval shape about 16 x 6 in (40 x 15 cm). Spread one-sixth of the cheese sauce down the middle, leaving a 1¼ in (3 cm) border around the edge. Sprinkle on some dried oregano and sesame seeds and top with a layer of leeks, then season with flaky salt. Fold in the sides as shown on page 61, and pinch the ends together really well so that the pide doesn't unravel during baking.

Slide your pide onto a very flat baking sheet, then slide it onto the preheated baking tray or pizza stone. Bake for 10–12 minutes, or until golden brown and crisp on the outside. Remove and brush the sides with the melted butter. Add a line of crispy potatoes down the middle, then sprinkle on some tulum cheese. Make 5 more in the same way.

MEAT

BARBECUED CHICKEN WINGS WITH GARLIC & KAYSERI PASTIRMA DRESSING

SERVES 4

⅔ cup (150 ml) extra-virgin olive oil, plus extra for the wings

3 garlic cloves, thinly sliced

8 slices Kayseri pastirma, sliced into ½ in (1 cm) strips

1 tablespoon thyme leaves

3½ tablespoons sherry vinegar

12 chicken wings, jointed into 2 pieces

small bunch of flat leaf parsley, leaves shredded

flaky sea salt and freshly ground black pepper

Chicken wings are one of my absolute favorite foods. More and more restaurants are serving them in different guises, and this is my take on them. Kayseri pastirma is a type of really delicious air-dried beef coated in *çemen* (a Turkish spice paste, see page 199), and it's worth tracking down in your local Turkish supermarket. If you can't find it, Spanish *cecina* would be a good alternative, or you could use another cured meat, such as chorizo or salami, although the flavors wouldn't be quite the same. This dressing works very well with lots of things; in the restaurant we also use it with shellfish such as mussels and clams.

Heat a barbecue until the coals turn grey. Alternatively, heat a grill or broiler until medium-hot.

———

Pour the olive oil into a small pan, add the garlic, and cook over medium heat until it starts to turn golden brown. Add the pastirma and cook until it starts to turn crispy, then add the thyme and sherry vinegar. Remove from the heat, pour into a large bowl, and leave to cool.

———

Coat the chicken wings in a little olive oil and season with salt and pepper. Cook on the grill or under the broiler for about 15 minutes, turning them every 1–2 minutes to ensure even cooking. Once they are golden brown and cooked through, remove from the heat and immediately put them in the bowl with the dressing. Add the parsley, give it all a good toss, and serve sprinkled with a little extra sea salt over the top.

CHICKEN LIVERS WITH GARLIC, ROSEMARY, CUMIN & DATE BUTTER ON TOAST

If you've already made the Medjool Date Butter (on page 186), this is a really quick and simple dish to throw together. The sweet, buttery sauce complements the iron-rich flavor of the chicken livers.

Toast the bread, either in a toaster or under a hot broiler, then set aside.

———

Heat the olive oil in a large frying pan over high heat and add the chicken livers. Sauté them for 1–2 minutes if you like them pink in the middle; if you prefer them cooked through, sauté for 4–5 minutes. Add the garlic, rosemary, and cumin and cook for another minute or so, or until the garlic starts to brown.

———

Remove the pan from the heat and add the date butter, according to taste. Gently stir until melted, then season with salt. Add the parsley and divide the mixture between the slices of toast.

SERVES 4

4 slices crusty white bread

2 tablespoons olive oil

1 lb 2 oz (500 g) chicken livers, trimmed and sinews removed

2 garlic cloves, thinly sliced

1 large sprig of rosemary, finely chopped

1 teaspoon ground cumin

2–3 heaped tablespoons Medjool Date Butter (see page 186)

small handful flat leaf parsley leaves, chopped

flaky sea salt

SALAD OF BAHARAT-ROAST DUCK WITH FETA, SUMAC ONIONS, POACHED FIGS & SALTED WALNUTS

I started out using *baharat* only in bread, but soon discovered how versatile this spice mixture is, and now use it in all sorts of dishes, including meat and fish recipes. If you don't have time to make your own using the recipe in this book, you can buy it from most Turkish supermarkets.

Preheat the oven to 400°F (200°C). Alternatively, if you have a barbecue that can cook things slowly, cook it on that for extra flavor.

Rub the duck with a little olive oil, then the baharat and salt. Place it upside down in a roasting pan and roast for 1 hour. Carefully drain off any excess oil from the pan and turn the duck over. Return to the oven for 1 more hour. Remove the duck and leave it to rest and cool a little. Reduce the oven temperature to 325°F (160°C).

Meanwhile, put the water in a small pan, add the sugar, star anise, and vinegar, and bring to a boil. Continue boiling to reduce the liquid by half. Add the figs, cut-side down, and cook gently for 4–5 minutes, or until they collapse just a little. Remove the figs and leave them to cool to room temperature.

To make the walnuts, whisk the egg white with the confectioner's sugar, salt, and some black pepper until a little frothy. Add the walnuts and coat well. Place on a baking tray lined with parchment paper and bake for 5–10 minutes, or until crisp and golden.

In a small bowl, mix together the onion and sumac with a pinch of salt. Massage them together a little and set aside. Tear the duck into pieces; it is up to you whether you would like it off the bone or not. Season the duck with salt.

Place the salad greens in a serving bowl along with the figs, mint leaves, onions, and feta, and mix gently. To serve, place a few pieces of duck on a plate, add some salad, and scatter over some walnuts. Drizzle over some olive oil and a squeeze of lemon to finish.

SERVES 4–6

1 free-range duck, giblets removed

extra-virgin olive oil, for rubbing and drizzling

2 tablespoons baharat (see page 193; also available in Turkish supermarkets)

⅔ cup (150 ml) water

¼ cup (1¾ oz/50 g) sugar

1 star anise

1½ tablespoons sherry vinegar or red wine vinegar

4 figs, cut in half

1 red onion, thinly sliced

2 tablespoons sumac

about 7 cups (5½ oz/150 g) mixed salad greens

leaves from 4 sprigs of mint

4¼ oz (120 g) Turkish white cheese or feta

1 lemon

flaky sea salt and freshly ground black pepper

FOR THE WALNUTS

1 large egg white

2½ tablespoons confectioner's sugar

1 teaspoon flaky sea salt

freshly ground black pepper

1¼ cups (4½ oz/125 g) walnuts

GRILLED QUAILS WITH A PALM SUGAR, SUMAC & OREGANO GLAZE

This was one of the first recipes I created when working for Peter Gordon at The Providores. I'd never cooked with palm sugar before I worked there and it was really exciting to experiment with this new ingredient. The birds are definitely best cooked on the barbecue, but if the weather isn't on your side, you can also cook them under a broiler.

Heat a barbecue until the coals have turned grey, or preheat a grill or broiler.

—

Mix together the palm sugar, sumac, oregano, and olive oil. Pour half the mixture over the quails and leave to marinate for at least 1 hour. Season the quails with salt and pepper and place them on the barbecue or under the broiler skin-side down. Make sure the coals are not too hot, or you may burn the skin. After 1 minute, turn the quails over, then turn every minute or so until they are cooked to your liking. I like to keep mine a little pink, so I cook them for 6–8 minutes. Just before removing them, brush with the remaining marinade and cook for another minute.

—

Remove the quails from the barbecue and leave to rest for about 5 minutes. Serve with the caper dressing.

SERVES 4

2 tablespoons palm sugar, pounded finely using a mortar and pestle

2 tablespoons sumac

1 tablespoon dried oregano

6 tablespoons (90 ml) extra-virgin olive oil

4 quails, spatchcocked

flaky sea salt and freshly ground black pepper

Caper Dressing (see page 194), to serve

CHILI-GARLIC GLAZED CHICKEN WITH ZA'ATAR CRUMBS

This recipe was designed for the press launch of Oklava, held on a rooftop in London. Conscious of the press's power to make or break a new restaurant, I was keen to create the best chicken dish I could, something that would stick in the memory of the journalists and critics attending. Torn between developing a smoky barbecued chicken and a crispy fried chicken, I came up with this recipe, which combines the best of both. It's sticky, smoky, crispy, and thoroughly messy to eat, especially if, as I do, you prefer to get in there with your hands. Although the recipe tells you how to make this in the oven, it's really best cooked over a barbecue for added smokiness, so if the sun is shining, get outside and cook al fresco. Serve with Lime Mayonnaise (see page 188).

SERVES 4–6

1 medium free-range chicken, cut into 10 pieces through the bone

olive oil, for drizzling

1 lime, cut into wedges

FOR THE BRINE

4¼ cups (1 liter) cold water

3 tablespoons fine salt

1 teaspoon sweet smoked paprika

FOR THE GLAZE

3 red chili peppers

15 small garlic cloves

generous 1½ cups (11½ oz/ 325 g) palm sugar

3 tablespoons Turkish hot pepper paste (açi biber salçasi)

¾ cup (175 ml) cider vinegar

FOR THE ZA'ATAR CRUMBS

scant 1 cup (2¾ oz/80 g) za'atar

3 tablespoons sesame seeds, lightly toasted

2½ tablespoons sumac

3¾ cups (10½ oz/300 g) dried breadcrumbs

flaky sea salt

Preheat the oven to 325°F (160°C). Remove the skin from all the chicken pieces except the wings. Put the skin on a baking tray and bake for about 30 minutes, or until golden and crisp, draining off the fat a few times during cooking. Once the skin has cooled, chop it finely. Turn the oven up to 475°F (240°C).

To make the brine, bring a scant 1 cup (200 ml) of the water to a boil with the salt and paprika. Tip it into a bowl and add the remaining cold water. Place the chicken pieces in a bowl, pour the brine over them, and refrigerate for 3 hours. Rinse the chicken under cold water and pat dry.

To make the glaze, roughly chop the chilies and garlic. Put them in a food processor and blend to a coarse purée. Put the palm sugar in a saucepan over medium heat and leave to caramelize. As soon as that happens, add the chili and garlic purée and hot pepper paste. Cook over medium heat for about 5 minutes. Finally, add the cider vinegar and continue to cook for 15–20 minutes, or until the glaze has a syrupy consistency.

To make the crumbs, combine the ingredients in a bowl and stir in the crispy chicken skin. Tip the mixture onto a large tray.

Put the chicken pieces on a large baking tray, well spaced, and drizzle with a little olive oil. Bake for about 15 minutes, or until two-thirds cooked. Remove from the oven and generously ladle the glaze over all the pieces. Return to the oven for 5 minutes, then remove and repeat the glazing process. Once the chicken is cooked through and well glazed, remove from the oven and put the pieces straight into the tray of za'atar crumbs. Coat them well and serve with the lime mayonnaise and wedges of lime on the side.

BEEF MEATBALLS IN SOUR CHERRY SAUCE WITH BULGUR PILAV

SERVES 6

1 lb 10 oz (750 g) ground beef

1 tablespoon baharat (see page 193; also available in Turkish supermarkets)

1 tablespoon Aleppo pepper flakes (pul biber)

fine salt

scant ½ cup (100 ml) extra-virgin olive oil

3 onions, chopped

2 tablespoons thyme, leaves removed

1 heaped teaspoon sweet pepper paste (tatli biber salçasi)

2 lb 4 oz (1 kg) red cherries, pitted

freshly squeezed juice of 1 lemon

3 tablespoons (1½ oz/40 g) cold unsalted butter, diced

small bunch of flat leaf parsley, chopped

flaky sea salt and freshly ground black pepper

FOR THE BULGUR PILAV

2 tablespoons extra-virgin olive oil

1 onion, chopped

1 tablespoon sweet pepper paste (tatli biber salçasi)

14 oz (400 g) canned tomatoes or 4 ripe tomatoes, chopped

1¼ cups (300 ml) stock or water

1½ cups (7 oz/200 g) coarse bulgur

fine salt

FOR THE FENNEL YOGURT

6 heaped tablespoons Turkish or Greek yogurt

1 tablespoon ground fennel

I first had this dish at Ciya Sofrasi in Istanbul, where the chef is known for recreating Ottoman dishes and incorporating wild ingredients into his food. This is my version of a classic. If you can't find fresh cherries, frozen will work well too. And if you can't find *tatli biber salçasi*, a type of Turkish sweet pepper paste, use tomato paste instead.

Start by mixing the ground beef with the baharat and pepper flakes and season with fine salt. Cook a little in a frying pan to check the seasoning, then adjust the mixture as necessary. Knead the mixture very well, then shape it into small meatballs about ¾ in (2 cm) in diameter. Chill until needed.

———

Heat the olive oil in a large shallow saucepan over medium heat and add the onions. Gently cook until soft, about 15 minutes. Add the thyme leaves and sweet pepper paste and continue to cook for 2 minutes. Now add the meatballs, half the cherries, and enough water to come halfway up the meatballs. Season with salt and pepper, give it a gentle stir, then cover and turn the heat right down. Cook for 30 minutes, stirring occasionally.

———

Meanwhile, make the bulgur pilav. Heat the olive oil in a small saucepan, add the onion, and cook gently over medium heat for about 10 minutes. Add the sweet pepper paste and cook for 1 more minute. Add the tomatoes, stock or water, bulgur, and a little fine salt. Stir well, increase the heat, and bring to a boil. Turn the heat right down, then cover and cook for 8–10 minutes, or until the liquid is absorbed. Remove from the heat, place a piece of paper towel directly on the bulgur, and put the lid on again. Set aside.

———

Mix together the yogurt and ground fennel. Season with flaky salt.

———

To finish the meatballs, add the remaining cherries, lemon juice, and butter. Cook for 5–10 minutes, or until you have a nice sauce consistency. Turn the heat off and add the parsley. Check the seasoning and serve with the pilav and fennel yogurt.

VEAL SHISH & ONION SALAD FLATBREAD WITH CHARRED SIVRI BIBER RELISH & YOGURT

For many people, veal remains a dirty word. Pasture-raised or rose veal from dairy farm bull calves is, however, an ethically sourced, high-welfare product with a delicate flavor. It's perfect in this flatbread recipe. I like to cook everything on a barbecue, but you can use a hot grill pan if you prefer. The breads could even be cooked in an oven preheated to 475°F (240°C).

Put the veal in a bowl with the red pepper flakes, cumin, oregano, and half the olive oil. Leave it to marinate in the refrigerator for a minimum of 2 hours, preferably overnight.

———

Heat a barbecue until the coals turn grey or preheat your grill pan or oven.

———

If you are making your own flatbreads, punch down the dough and divide it into 8–10 equal pieces, depending on how big you want to make them. Lightly flour a work surface and roll out one piece at a time into a long oval shape about ¹/₈ in (4 mm) thick. As you roll them, place directly on the hot barbecue rack, grill pan, or oven shelf (make sure the bars aren't too wide apart) and cook for about 1 minute on each side, or until a little puffed up and charred. Set aside and keep warm.

———

To make the relish, put the peppers on the barbecue (or in the grill pan) and cook, turning them occasionally, until blackened all over. Remove and leave to cool. Once cool enough to handle, tear the tops off and strip away most of the skin, but don't remove all the charred bits. Chop the flesh into small pieces. Place in a bowl and mix with the scallions, cilantro, lemon juice, and olive oil. Season with salt and pepper.

———

To make the onion salad, separate the onion layers, push them onto metal skewers, and place on the barbecue. Cook for 2–3 minutes, turning now and then, until charred on both sides. Remove from the skewer and put them in a bowl with the pomegranate molasses, turnip juice, olive oil, parsley, and sumac. Season with salt and pepper and give it a good mix.

———

Finally, thread the veal pieces onto metal skewers and grill for about 3 minutes on each side, or until golden brown. Season them with fine salt during cooking. Place the skewers straight on the flatbreads to rest and release their juices for 5 minutes. To serve, spread some yogurt on a flatbread and top with the veal, onion salad, and pepper relish.

SERVES 6

1 lb 10 oz (750 g) rose veal shoulder, leg, or sirloin, cut into 1¼ in (3 cm) cubes

1 tablespoon Urfa red pepper flakes (isot biber)

1 tablespoon ground cumin

1 tablespoon dried oregano

scant ½ cup (100 ml) extra-virgin olive oil

1 quantity Pide dough (see page 60) or 4 good-quality flatbreads

flour, for dusting

fine salt

¼ cup (60 ml) Turkish or Greek yogurt

flaky sea salt and freshly ground pepper

FOR THE SIVRI BIBER RELISH

8 hot Turkish peppers (sivri biber; use green chilies if you can't find them)

4 scallions, thinly sliced

small bunch of cilantro, leaves and stalks, chopped

freshly squeezed juice of 1 lemon

3½ tablespoons extra-virgin olive oil

FOR THE ONION SALAD

2 onions, quartered

2 tablespoons pomegranate molasses

4 teaspoons turnip juice (salgam)

3½ tablespoons extra-virgin olive oil

small bunch of flat leaf parsley, leaves only

1 tablespoon sumac

STEAK TANTUNI WITH RED ONION, PEPPER & PARSLEY SALAD

SERVES 2

2 tablespoons Turkish or Greek yogurt

1 tablespoon Turkish hot pepper paste (açi biber salçasi)

1 tablespoon extra-virgin olive oil

2 round steaks, about 9 oz (250 g) each

2–3 tablespoons sunflower oil

1 Turkish loaf (somun) or a small baguette

1–2 teaspoons Urfa red pepper flakes (isot biber)

1–2 teaspoons sweet smoked paprika

2 plum tomatoes, peeled and diced

2 long green Turkish peppers (Charleston peppers; use ordinary peppers if you can't find them), sliced

flaky sea salt

FOR THE SALAD

1 small red onion, thinly sliced

2 tablespoons sumac

small bunch of flat leaf parsley, leaves only, shredded

I came up with this recipe for Soho Food Feast, a fundraising fête held every year at Soho Parish Primary School in central London. A number of London restaurants set up food stalls at this amazing event, which also features live music, a raffle, and the always-hilarious children's vegetable sculpture competition. *Tantuni*, from the port city of Mersin in southeast Turkey, is traditionally made with boiled beef or chicken but I prefer to use fried steak as a Turkish take on the classic steak sandwich.

Mix the yogurt with the hot pepper paste and olive oil. Smear this all over the steaks and leave to marinate in the refrigerator for 2 hours (remove them 30 minutes before cooking).

———

Heat 1½ tablespoons of the sunflower oil in a large frying pan. Season the steaks with salt and fry for 2–3 minutes on each side, until a caramelized crust forms. Remove from the pan and leave to rest for 10 minutes. Clean the pan with paper towels and set aside.

———

Meanwhile, make the salad. Mix the onion with the sumac and parsley. Season with flaky sea salt and set aside until needed.

———

Dice the steaks into roughly ½ in (1 cm) pieces. Split the bread lengthways, not quite cutting all the way through, and trim it so that it will eventually fit into the frying pan. Heat the remaining oil in the empty pan until it is very hot. Add the diced meat, red pepper flakes, and paprika, and fry for 2 minutes, then add about 3 tablespoons water and a little more salt. Scrape any sticky bits off the bottom of the pan, then put the bread cut-side down on top of the meat and push it right down so it soaks up all the juices from the pan.

———

To serve, put the bread on a chopping board and scoop all the meat onto it. Top with the onion salad, tomatoes, and peppers. Season with a little extra salt, then cut in half and serve.

ARTICHOKE & BEEF DOLMA

This is another of my mother's recipes, and a regular feature on our Sunday dinner table. While writing this book, I've often called my mom to check the ingredients and techniques of some of her favorite dishes. At times this has been difficult—the recipes are second nature to her, so she'd tell me to put "some" of this, "a bit" of that, and "not too much" of the other. Mom doesn't use measurements, so getting to the end result you see in this book hasn't always been straightforward. With this dish, though, it can be particularly difficult to get the quantities right, since each artichoke will be a different size, making it tricky to know exactly how much filling you'll need. I always make extra, since this mixture also works well stuffed into potatoes, peppers, zucchinis, or just about any vegetable you fancy.

8 globe artichokes

freshly squeezed juice of 2–3 lemons

3½ tablespoons extra-virgin olive oil

2 onions, diced

2 lb 4 oz (1 kg) ground beef

1 tablespoon tomato paste

14 oz (400 g) canned tomatoes, or 4 fresh tomatoes, chopped

1⅓ cups (9 oz/250 g) long-grain rice, rinsed

large bunch of flat leaf parsley, chopped (a little bit of stalk is good)

8 large slices tomato

flaky sea salt and freshly ground black pepper

Cut the stalks off the artichokes and remove the chokes using a small knife and a spoon, as shown in the photographs. Put the hollowed artichokes in a bowl of water with the juice of 1 lemon.

——

Heat the oil in a large pan, add the onions, and cook gently for about 15 minutes, or until translucent. Add the ground beef and cook until it takes on a little color, about 15 minutes. Break up the meat thoroughly as it cooks. Add the tomato paste and tomatoes and cook the mixture over medium heat for a further 20 minutes. Season with salt and pepper. Add the rice and cook for another 5 minutes. Turn the heat off, add the parsley and the juice of 1 lemon (or more if you like it very lemony), and leave to cool. Meanwhile. preheat the oven to 375°F (190°C).

——

Once the filling has cooled, drain the artichokes and pat dry with paper towels. Spoon the filling into the hollows, then place the artichokes on a baking tray that holds them snugly. Top each one with a slice of tomato. Fill the tray halfway up with water, cover tightly with foil, and bake for about 1 hour, or until the rice is cooked through. Remove the foil and bake for a further 10 minutes. Set aside and allow to cool a little before serving.

ÇEMEN-BRAISED SHORT RIBS
WITH BROWN BUTTER BREAD SAUCE

Çemen is a Turkish spice paste used to make Kayseri pastirma, but it is also served as a mezze to be spread onto bread. If you don't want to make your own (see page 199), you can buy it from a Turkish supermarket. This dish is delicious served with Tomato-Pomegranate Salad (see page 16) to cut through the richness of the sauce. I also recommend serving it with melted Chili Butter (see page 186), as shown here.

SERVES 4

4 beef short ribs on the bone, about 4½ in (12 cm) long

1 onion, sliced

2 tablespoons çemen

½ quantity Chili Butter (see page 186), to serve (optional)

FOR THE BREAD SAUCE

2 tablespoons sunflower oil

1 shallot, diced

2 garlic cloves, grated

7 tablespoons (3½ oz/100 g) unsalted butter

about 1½ cups (3½ oz/100 g) fresh white breadcrumbs

generous 2 cups (500 ml) milk

⅓ cup (80 ml) heavy cream

flaky sea salt

Preheat the oven to 350°F (180°C). Put the short ribs in a roasting pan that fits them snugly and tuck the onion around them. Whisk the çemen with a little water to form a loose paste. Pour it into the pan and top up with just enough water to submerge the ribs. Cover with foil and bake for 3–4 hours, or until the meat is just coming away from the bone.

Meanwhile, make the bread sauce. Heat half the oil in a pan over low heat, add the shallot and garlic, and cook for about 5 minutes, or until softened. In a separate pan, melt the butter over medium heat and keep cooking until it turns a nut-brown color. Strain it through a fine sieve lined with paper towels. Add the breadcrumbs to the shallots, followed by the milk. Gently cook over low heat, stirring until thickened. Add the cream and season with salt. Finally, whisk in the browned butter. If you prefer, you could blend the sauce until completely smooth.

Once the ribs are cooked, pour the cooking liquid into a pan and reduce over high heat until it reaches a gravy-like consistency. This might take a while, depending how much liquid you have. Remove and discard any bones or gristle from the meat. Wrap each rib tightly in plastic wrap and leave to cool in the refrigerator. Meanwhile, melt the chili butter, if using, and keep warm.

Once cool, cut each rib into 5 slices. Heat the remaining sunflower oil in a large frying pan. Add the rib slices and fry on each side until browned. Add some of the reduced meat sauce and turn the heat down. Cook the slices in the sauce until glazed (you might need to do this in a few batches).

To serve, reheat the bread sauce if necessary. Spoon it onto plates, place the beef on the sauce, and add a little drizzle of extra sauce over the top. Pour over some warm chili butter, if using.

FRIED BEEF KÖFTE

SERVES 4–6

4 potatoes, finely grated
(any white potato is fine, but
I like Cyprus potatoes)

1 lb 5 oz (600 g) ground beef

2 small or 1 large onion, finely
chopped

small bunch of flat leaf
parsley, finely chopped

1 large egg

2¼–3 cups (5½–7 oz/
150–200 g) fresh white
breadcrumbs (from a white
crusty loaf, crusts removed)

vegetable oil, for frying

fine salt and freshly ground
black pepper

This is a classic Cypriot *köfte*, just like my mom makes them. The addition of potato keeps them really moist in the middle and crispy on the outside. At home we would always have them with Turkish-style rice or Cyprus potato fries and a big bowl of chopped salad. When we have these on the menu in the restaurant I always serve them with Tomato Relish (see page 189) as a dip on the side. For best results, cook one *köfte* to check the seasoning before shaping and frying the rest.

Put the grated potatoes in a clean dish towel and squeeze with your hands to get rid of any excess liquid. Transfer to a large bowl and add all the remaining ingredients, except the oil, and season with salt and pepper. Knead the mixture for about 1 minute.

———

Pour enough oil into a frying pan to fill it no more than one-third full and place over medium heat. Alternatively, heat the oil in a deep-fryer.

———

Shape the beef mixture into köftes—either short, stumpy oval sausages (as is traditional) or small balls. It's easier to do this with damp hands. When the oil reaches 350°F (180°C), or a small cube of bread added to the oil sizzles immediately, you can start frying.

———

Add as many köftes as your pan can hold, leaving a ¾ in (2 cm) gap between them. Cook until they have taken on a nice dark brown color, then flip them over and cook the other side. Remove and drain on paper towels.

———

Continue to cook in batches until the mixture is used up. If you want to eat the köftes all at the same time, earlier batches can be reheated in a low oven. They can also be eaten warm or even cold.

SPICED BEEF & BULGUR KÖFTES

This is my take on a traditional Cypriot dish that I learned from one of my mom's friends. Traditionally, the dough is made with only bulgur and water, but getting the consistency right can be challenging, which is why I've added eggs, flour, and olive oil. You can add different spices and herbs to the meat to your liking, but it's important not to add more wet ingredients, or you are likely to end up with a cracked casing where the juices have run into the dough.

Start by making the dough. In a large, deep tray, combine the bulgur and fine salt and add enough of the water to cover the bulgur by about ½ in (1 cm); the wheat will start absorbing it immediately but you don't need to add more. Mix thoroughly, then cover with a clean cloth and leave to absorb all the liquid; this will take about 30 minutes.

——

Meanwhile, to make the filling, heat 2 tablespoons of the oil in a frying pan over medium heat, add the onions, and cook until lightly browned. Remove from the pan. Carefully wipe the pan out with paper towels and return it to high heat.

——

Add the remaining olive oil and the beef, breaking it up in the pan. Fry until it has browned all over and any excess moisture has evaporated. This will take about 15 minutes. Return the onion to the pan and season with salt and pepper.

——

Now add the spices and cook for a few more minutes. Add the vinegar and sugar and cook for another minute. Remove from the heat and stir in the parsley. Check the seasoning and leave the meat to cool.

——

To finish the dough, add the egg, olive oil, and ¼ cup (1 oz/30 g) flour to the soaked bulgur and knead by hand or using a stand mixer with the paddle attachment for at least 5–10 minutes, or until you can form it into a ball without it sticking to your hands. If you feel the mixture is too wet, add a little more flour.

——

Heat the oil in a deep-fryer to 350°F (180°C). Alternatively, place a deep frying pan over high heat and add enough sunflower oil to cover the köftes. When hot enough, a small cube of bread added to the oil should sizzle immediately.

——

To shape the köftes, break off a piece of dough a bit bigger than a golf ball and roll into a ball. Using slightly wet hands, poke your finger in and start turning the dough, shaping it into a long pocket with ¹/₃ in (8 mm) thick walls. Keep the top end a bit wider so that it is easier to stuff. Spoon in some of the beef filling, leaving about ½ in (1 cm) empty at the top. Now close off the end and ensure there are no gaps in your dough. If there are any cracks, remold, adding extra dough if needed, and smooth it over with damp hands.

——

Carefully place a few köftes at a time in the hot oil and fry for about 5 minutes, or until dark golden brown. Repeat the process until all the mixture is used up. Serve with lemon wedges to squeeze into the filling.

MAKES 16–20

sunflower oil, for frying

1 lemon, cut into wedges

yogurt with a drizzle of pomegranate molasses, to serve (optional)

FOR THE DOUGH

1½ cups (9 oz/250 g) fine bulgur

1 teaspoon fine salt

about 3⅓ cups (800 ml) boiling water

1 medium egg

1 tablespoon extra-virgin olive oil

¼–½ cup (1–2 oz/30–60 g) all-purpose flour

FOR THE FILLING

¼ cup (60 ml) olive oil

2 onions, chopped

1 lb 2 oz (500 g) ground beef

1 teaspoon ground cumin

1 teaspoon ground coriander

1 teaspoon sweet smoked paprika

1 tablespoon sherry vinegar

1 teaspoon sugar

small bunch of flat leaf parsley, finely shredded (a little stalk is good)

flaky sea salt and freshly ground black pepper

SPICED BRAISED OXTAIL WITH SHALLOTS

Oxtail is a delicious but under-used cut: when cooked slowly, it produces soft, melting meat that is perfect for this hearty dish. A tablespoon of *açi biber salçasi* (hot pepper paste) adds warmth, but if you're not a fan, replace it with more tomato paste. I like to serve this stew with mashed potatoes or a good loaf of crusty white bread to mop up the juices.

Preheat the oven to 350°F (180°C). Place the oil in a Dutch oven or ovensafe casserole dish over high heat. Season the oxtail and dust it in the flour. Add it to the dish and cook until dark brown on both sides. Remove and set aside. If the meat has released a lot of oil, remove some of it from the pan.

———

Add the whole shallots to the dish and turn the heat down to medium. Gently cook until golden brown, about 10 minutes. Add the bay leaf, spices, tomato paste, and pepper paste and cook for another 5 minutes. Add the red wine and cook to reduce by half. Return the oxtail to the dish and add just enough water to cover it. Put the lid on and place in the oven for 2–3 hours, or until the meat is falling off the bone.

———

Remove the oxtail and place the dish over high heat to reduce the cooking liquid to a thick sauce. Return the oxtail to the dish, check the seasoning, and serve.

SERVES 2–4

2 tablespoons sunflower oil

4 slices oxtail, about 2 in (5 cm) thick

1 tablespoon all-purpose flour

12 round shallots

1 bay leaf

1 teaspoon ground cumin

1 teaspoon ground cinnamon

1 star anise

1 tablespoon tomato paste

1 tablespoon Turkish hot pepper paste (açi biber salçasi)

½ cup (120 ml) red wine

flaky sea salt and freshly ground black pepper

FRIED BEEF & ALLSPICE KÖFTES

SERVES 4–6

1 cup (250 ml) water

⅓ cup (2¼ oz/60 g) long-grain rice, rinsed in warm water

sunflower oil, for frying

2 onions, chopped

1 lb 2 oz (500 g) ground beef

1 teaspoon ground allspice

1 teaspoon freshly ground black pepper

3 large eggs

all-purpose flour, for dusting

fine salt

This dish is called *kadin budu koftesi* in Turkish, which means "ladies' thighs meatballs." I've heard that this is because the shape of these *köftes* resemble female legs, although whether this is truth or folktale, I really couldn't say. But I can tell you that they work well as a part of a mezze spread, or served alongside a nice mixed salad.

Put the measured water in a small saucepan and bring to a boil. Add the rice, season with a little salt, and boil for 10–15 minutes, or until just cooked. Drain and set aside to cool.

———

Heat a little oil in a frying pan, add the onions, and cook gently over medium heat for about 10 minutes, or until soft. Add half the ground beef and continue to cook for 10–15 minutes, or until lightly browned. Set aside to cool.

———

In a large bowl, combine the remaining ground beef with the rice, allspice, black pepper, 1 egg, and the cooked meat. Season with salt and knead for about 5–10 minutes, or until the ingredients are well incorporated and form a ball. Fry a little piece to check the seasoning, then adjust the remaining raw mixture as necessary. Divide it into 14 equal pieces, and shape each into an oval patty.

———

Heat a shallow depth of oil in a large frying pan. Beat the remaining eggs in a bowl. Dust each patty in flour, coat in the egg, and place in the hot oil. Fry for 1½ minutes, or until golden on each side. Drain on paper towels and season with a little fine salt.

RABBIT FRITTERS

SERVES 6–8

1 rabbit, farmed or wild, jointed into 8 pieces

4 onions, chopped

scant 1 cup (200 ml) red wine vinegar

scant 1 cup (200 ml) extra-virgin olive oil

4 sprigs of thyme

1 sprig of rosemary

4 sprigs of flat leaf parsley, chopped

4 sprigs of tarragon, chopped

sunflower oil, for frying

flaky sea salt and freshly ground black pepper

FOR THE BATTER

2 cups (9 oz/250 g) all-purpose flour, plus extra for rolling

1 tablespoon (⅓ oz/10 g) instant yeast (about 1½ envelopes)

1 teaspoon sugar

2 tablespoons nigella seeds

about 1¾ cups (400 ml) sparkling water

fine salt

I discovered *lalangi* (rabbit fritters) while chatting to one of my mom's friends about Cypriot food. Traditionally, this is a very simple dish in which you boil a whole rabbit in water and coat the picked meat in batter. The cooking method I use comes from my mom. Back in Cyprus, my dad used to go out hunting and bring back wild hares and rabbits. Mom would use vinegar and herbs to tame the strong flavor of the wild meat, a technique that I've adopted for many of my gamey dishes. Serve with Black Olive & Pepper Tapenade (see page 189).

Preheat the oven to 350°F (180°C). Put the rabbit in a roasting pan with 2 chopped onions, half the vinegar, half the olive oil, and the thyme and rosemary. Season with salt and pepper. Cover the pan with foil and roast for 90 minutes, or until the rabbit is falling off the bone. Remove and set aside to cool.

Meanwhile, put the remaining onions with the remaning olive oil in a small saucepan over medium heat and cook gently until caramelized; this will take 10–15 minutes. Add the remaining vinegar and allow it to bubble until there is almost no liquid left. Leave the onions to cool.

———

Once the rabbit is cool enough to handle, pick all the meat off the bones and shred it up a little. Drain off any juices and onions from the rabbit and cook these gently in a small pan until there is almost no liquid left. Add it to the caramelized onions.

———

Season the rabbit meat and add the parsley, tarragon, and onions. Mix it well, then shape the rabbit mixture into small balls about 1¼ in (3 cm) in diameter.

———

To make the batter, put the flour in a bowl along with the yeast, sugar, and nigella seeds. Gradually add the sparkling water, whisking continously. You are aiming for quite a thick batter, like one you would make for fish, so you might not need all the water. Finish by adding the salt and leave it to rest for 30 minutes.

———

Heat the oil in a deep-fryer to 350°F (180°C). Alternatively, heat a 1½ in (4 cm) depth of oil in a frying pan over high heat. When hot enough, a small cube of bread added to the oil should sizzle immediately.

———

In batches of however many will comfortably fit in your fryer or pan, roll the balls of rabbit in flour, dip them in the batter, then carefully add to the hot oil. Fry until golden and crispy. Remove and drain on paper towels and season with fine salt. Repeat with the rest of the mixture.

CRISPY POMEGRANATE-GLAZED LAMB WITH YOGURT

Having initially created this dish in my days as head chef at Kopapa, I have since developed it as presented here. It was born out of my love for lamb, pomegranate molasses, and yogurt, and started out as lamb ribs. However, after a chef overcooked them and they all fell off the bone, I decided it was even better as lots of bits of crispy lamb. At the restaurant we press the lamb under a weight overnight to help with portioning, but you don't have to do that if you don't want to; it is just as delicious as randomly shaped crispy chunks. The lamb is best prepared a day in advance.

Preheat the oven to 350°F (180°C). Place the lamb breast, onion, and bay leaf in a large roasting pan or ovenproof casserole dish. Add enough water to cover the lamb by about ¾ in (2 cm). Cover with foil or a lid and roast for about 3 hours. The lamb is ready when you can pull the bones away without any resistance. Set the lamb aside to cool, reserving the cooking liquid.

———

When the lamb is cool enough to handle, but not completely cold, remove as much meat as possible, discarding the bones and any cartilage. Place the meat in the fridge until the fat has set—preferably overnight. To achieve the neat cubes shown here, layer the lamb in a shallow rectangular tray—it should be tightly packed. Put another tray on top and weigh it down to press the lamb into shape. The next day, cut the meat into ¾ in (2 cm) cubes.

———

To make the sauce, preheat the oven to 375°F (190°C). Put all the spices in a small roasting pan and toast them on the middle shelf for about 6 minutes. Discard any fat on the surface of the reserved cooking liquid, then place in a small pan with the toasted spices, pomegranate molasses, cider vinegar, and sugar. Allow this to simmer, stirring occasionally, until it has the consistency of cream, then strain off and discard the spices.

———

Put the diced lamb in a dry frying pan over medium-high heat and fry until crispy all over, turning occasionally and seasoning with sea salt as you go. Be aware that a lot of fat will come out and the pan may spit at you, so take care. The pieces of lamb will break up a little in the pan, but that's fine. You want some bits that are super crispy and some bits that are soft in the middle; this can take anywhere from 8–12 minutes. Transfer the lamb to a colander to drain, discarding the excess fat. Season with flaky sea salt.

———

To serve, place the yogurt in individual bowls or one big bowl. Place the lamb on top, pour over as much sauce as you like, and sprinkle with the herbs.

SERVES 4

1 bone-in lamb breast, about 4 lb 8 oz (2 kg)—ask your butcher to cut it into 4 or 5 pieces to make it more manageable

1 large onion, thickly sliced

1 bay leaf

flaky sea salt

FOR THE SAUCE

¼ teaspoon black peppercorns

¼ teaspoon fennel seeds

¼ teaspoon coriander seeds

1 cinnamon stick

4 cloves

scant ½ cup (100 ml) pomegranate molasses

3½ tablespoons cider vinegar

2 tablespoons dark brown sugar

TO SERVE

4 heaped tablespoons Turkish or Greek yogurt

4 sprigs of mint, finely shredded

4 sprigs of flat leaf parsley, finely shredded

QUINCE & ROSEMARY-GLAZED LAMB

SERVES 4

3½ oz (100 g) quince paste (membrillo)

1 sprig of rosemary, stalks removed

1 tablespoon sherry vinegar

2 tablespoons sunflower oil

4 lamb sirloin chops, 7 oz (200 g) each, fat cap lightly scored

1 heaped tablespoon unsalted butter

flaky sea salt and freshly ground black pepper

I have to restrain myself from putting too many lamb dishes on the menu. As a Turk, I guess this love affair with lamb is quite natural. Lamb sirloin chop is an underused cut, which is a great shame since it is full of flavor. Try to buy your lamb from a butcher, if you can. This recipe would work really well served with roast potatoes and vegetables, but it can also be served alongside other dishes for sharing. You could try the glaze with a leg of lamb instead—in which case preheat the oven to 400°F (200°C) and roast for 25 minutes for every 1 lb (450 g) of lamb. Increase the temperature to 425°F (220°C), and pour on the glaze. Return to the oven for 10 minutes, or until caramelized, basting halfway through the cooking time.

Preheat the oven to 425°F (220°C). In a small blender, process the quince paste, rosemary, sherry vinegar, and 3 tablespoons water until smooth.

———

Heat the oil in a large ovenproof frying pan over medium heat. Season the lamb pieces with salt and pepper and put them in the pan, fat-side down. Cook for about 5 minutes, or until golden. Increase the heat and turn them over. Brown them on all sides, then turn them fat-side down again. Transfer the pan to the oven and roast for 5 minutes. Turn the lamb pieces over and return to the oven for 3 minutes. Remove and allow to rest for at least 10 minutes. The meat will be pink in the middle; if you prefer it well cooked, just leave it in the oven for a bit longer.

———

Once the lamb has rested, put the pan over high heat. Add the lamb, about 3½ tablespoons of the glaze, and the butter. You can add all the glaze if you like this dish extra sticky, or save the rest to use another time; it keeps well in the fridge. Let the glaze bubble up, turning until it is well coated. Remove the lamb and leave to cool slightly. Once cool enough to handle, slice each piece into 4 or 5 slices. Pour over any pan juices and sprinkle over some flaky sea salt to serve.

SPICED FRIED CRISPY LAMB'S LIVER

SERVES 4

9 oz (250 g) lamb's liver, membranes removed

1 cup (250 ml) milk

1 tablespoon ground fennel

1 tablespoon ground cumin

1 tablespoon sweet smoked paprika

1 tablespoon Urfa red pepper flakes (isot biber)

1 cup (4½ oz/125 g) all-purpose flour

1 tablespoon fine salt, plus extra for seasoning

sunflower oil, for frying

Laura and I first tried this dish while in Turkey before the opening of Oklava. We had spent a lovely night at Arcadia vineyard, and on the way back to Istanbul our hosts took us to a restaurant in Edirne, close to the borders with Greece and Bulgaria. Edirne is famous for its thinly sliced fried lamb's liver and we were keen to try it out. Our hosts ordered what turned out to be huge plates of the dish, which I excitedly dug into, relishing the rich flavor. If you're an offal fan like me, you'll love this simple dish, which I've adapted with the addition of a few spices. If you can't find Urfa red pepper flakes, use regular red pepper flakes instead. Serve with tomatoes, raw onions, lettuce, bread, and Fried Dried Chili Yogurt (see page 199).

Slice the liver into very thin strips about ¹/₈ in (3 mm) thick. Soak it in the milk for about 1 hour. Mix all the spices together in a small bowl. Mix the flour with the measured salt.

———

Heat a ½ in (1 cm) depth of oil in a shallow frying pan over medium heat. Take the liver slices out of the milk in small batches and coat them thoroughly in the seasoned flour. You can place the liver slices in a sieve to shake off any excess flour.

———

Lower the slices into the hot oil, ensuring they are well separated, and fry for 1–2 minutes, or until crisp and golden. Drain on paper towels and season with salt and the spice mixture.

FAMILY KEBABS

Even if I've just eaten dinner, the smell of kebabs makes me hungry again—it is probably my favorite meal. I'm not talking kebabs from your local food cart, I'm talking about ones you will find, mostly on a Sunday, in pretty much every Turkish household.

Eating kebabs is a big social occasion. When I was growing up, I remember being excited when I knew we were having kebabs, not only because I loved them, but also because it meant that all my cousins would be coming over to play. Kebabs are cooked on a barbecue, and the ultimate barbecues are held on the beach. The beach is a 5-minute drive from where my grandparents live in Cyprus, and families gather there every weekend to have their own barbecue or order kebabs from one of the beach shacks. It's a day of pure indulgence for me, consisting of sea, sunshine, sand, and the smell of kebabs wafting from every direction. Here is what a typical barbecue at the Kiazim household consists of: Şeftali, Adana Köfte with Pita Bread, Spicy Tomato Sauce and Yogurt, Lamb Shish, Lamb Chops, Chicken Pieces, my Mom's Hummus and Pilav, Cyprus Potato Salad, and Shepherd's Salad.

LAMB SHISH

In our household we often use lamb leg meat for shish, but you could also use shoulder, depending on how much the fat content worries you. Dice the lamb into about ¾ in (2 cm) cubes, trimming it of any sinew and excessive fat (although a few cubes of fat skewered along with the meat is a good thing). Marinate the lamb for at least 2 hours, preferably overnight, in good olive oil and dried oregano (preferably wild oregano, known as kekik in Turkish, which has a more perfumed flavor). Place the meat on skewers and cook over very hot charcoals, seasoning with fine salt as you go.

LAMB CHOPS

You can grill lamb rib chops, which are delicious. I like getting in there and eating all the bits of meat off the bone. Grill the chops over hot coals, seasoning with fine salt as you go, and turning them regularly to ensure they cook evenly.

CHICKEN PIECES

Joint a chicken into 8–10 pieces through the bone (your butcher can do this for you). I prefer to leave the skin on. Marinate it in good olive oil, lemon, and dried oregano for at least 4 hours. Cook over medium-hot coals, seasoning with fine salt as you go, and turning it regularly to make sure the chicken cooks evenly and doesn't burn.

KEBAB MENU

ŞEFTALI (SEE PAGE 106)

ADANA KÖFTE WITH PITA BREAD, SPICY TOMATO SAUCE AND YOGURT (SEE PAGE 105)

LAMB SHISH (SEE BELOW)

LAMB CHOPS (SEE BELOW)

CHICKEN PIECES (SEE BELOW)

MOM'S HUMMUS (SEE PAGE 110)

MOM'S PILAV (SEE PAGE 110)

CYPRUS POTATO SALAD WITH ROMAINE LETTUCE, HERBS, SCALLIONS, LEMON & OLIVE OIL (SEE PAGE 113)

SHEPHERD'S SALAD (SEE PAGE 113)

ADANA KÖFTE WITH PITA BREAD, SPICY TOMATO SAUCE & YOGURT

SERVES 6

2 lb (900 g) ground lamb or beef

3½ oz (100 g) lamb suet (optional), frozen and finely grated

1 onion, finely chopped

large bunch of flat leaf parsley, finely chopped (a little stalk is good)

2 teaspoons fine salt, plus a little extra

6 pita breads

1 quantity Spicy Tomato Sauce (page 34), made without the bread

6 heaped tablespoons Turkish or Greek yogurt

freshly ground black pepper

This simple, classic kebab is named after the fifth largest city in Turkey. It works well as a meal in itself and is a favorite of my sister Sinem, who will sometimes light the barbecue mid-week just to make it. For an added bit of luxury, serve with Chili Butter (see page 186) drizzled over the top.

Start by making the köfte. Combine the meat, suet, onion, parsley, and salt. Add pepper to taste and knead well for 5–10 minutes. Divide into 3 oz (85 g) pieces and shape into small oval patties. Chill the köftes until needed.

Heat a barbecue until the coals turn grey, then grill the köftes over medium-hot coals, seasoning with a little fine salt and turning them regularly. If you have a grill basket for sandwiching fish on the barbecue, I would recommend using that. If not, just be careful when turning them over.

Grill the pita breads on the barbecue and cut them into strips, then add some tomato sauce, pile on the köftes, and top with yogurt.

ŞEFTALI

Şeftali was probably one of the first things I planned to put on the menu at Oklava, first because it's a Cypriot kebab, and second because it's my favorite! You must eat it with an onion salad, lavash or Turkish bread to absorb the juices, and lots of lemon. I have given specific measurements for the onion and parsley because for me it is very important to have the correct quantities, and every bunch of parsley or onion weighs a different amount.

Mix together the beef, onion, parsley, salt, pepper flakes, and lamb suet. Knead for 5–10 minutes, or until well combined. Divide the mixture into 3 oz (85 g) pieces and shape each one into a sausage about 2¾ in (7 cm) long.

To wrap the şeftali, stretch a large piece of caul fat over a chopping board. Place a sausage on one corner of the board and cut the caul fat around it, leaving a ¾ in (1.5 cm) margin on 3 sides and leaving it at least 4 in (10 cm) long on the fourth side. Roll the caul fat around the sausage one and a half times, tucking in the margins as you go. Repeat with the rest of the sausages.

Thread the sausages onto 2 large skewers, weaving them in and out to prevent them unraveling. Alternatively, if you have a grill basket for sandwiching fish on the barbecue, you can line them up in that. Cook over medium-hot coals, seasoning with a little fine salt during cooking, and turning them regularly.

MAKES 18

2 lb (900 g) ground beef

1 lb (450 g) onions, finely chopped

5 cups (10½ oz/300 g) finely chopped flat leaf parsley (a little bit of stalk is good)

2 teaspoons fine salt, plus a little extra

⅓ cup (1½ oz/40 g) Aleppo pepper flakes (pul biber)

7 oz (200 g) lamb suet, frozen and finely grated

4 lb 8 oz–6 lb 8 oz (2–3 kg) lamb caul fat, soaked in cold water with the juice of 1 lemon for 1 hour

MOM'S HUMMUS

Every Middle Eastern cook has their own recipe for making hummus and thinks theirs is the best. My mom's isn't fancy, but it's what I grew up with, so to me it is the best. She would always get me to taste it while she was making it and ask me, "More garlic? More lemon?" Feel free to be flexible with the recipe, adding more or less tahini, garlic, lemon, *pul biber*, or olive oil as you wish. I like it pretty lemony and garlicky.

Put the chickpeas, tahini, garlic, olive oil, pepper flakes, and 2 tablespoons of water in a food processor and blend to a coarse purée. Add the lemon juice and check the seasoning.

———

Place in your serving bowl and garnish with olive oil, sumac, and parsley.

SERVES 6–8

2 x 14 oz (400 g) cans chickpeas, drained and rinsed

about ¼ cup (2¾ oz/75 g) tahini

1-2 garlic cloves

2 tablespoons extra-virgin olive oil, plus extra for drizzling

½–1 teaspoon Aleppo pepper flakes (pul biber)

freshly squeezed juice of 1–2 lemons

sumac, to garnish

flat leaf parsley, chopped, to garnish

fine salt, to taste

MOM'S PILAV

Many people find cooking rice tricky, but the two top tips I learned from my mom work a treat every time: always rinse the rice really well, then follow the rule of two parts water to one part rice. Rice cooked like this was a staple in our household since it goes really well with stew-style dishes (known as *yahni* in Turkish).

Heat the oil in a medium saucepan, add the onion, and cook for a few minutes until softened. Add the broken vermicelli pieces and cook until slightly golden.

Add the rice and stir to coat in the oil for 1 minute.

———

Add the stock, season with salt, bring to a boil, and give it one last stir. Turn the heat down to a low simmer, then cover and cook for about 15 minutes, or just until the water has evaporated. Remove from the heat and uncover, place a few sheets of paper towel over the top, and put the lid back on. Leave to stand for 10 minutes before serving.

SERVES 6–8

1 tablespoon extra-virgin olive oil

1 small white onion, chopped

1⅓ cups (4½ oz/125 g) broken vermicelli pasta pieces

2¾ cups (1 lb 2 oz/500 g) long-grain rice, rinsed thoroughly in warm water

4¼ cups (1 liter) boiling chicken or vegetable stock (I always follow the rule of 1 part rice to 2 parts liquid)

fine salt

SHEPHERD'S SALAD

SERVES 6–8

4 plum tomatoes, cut into ½ in (1 cm) cubes

1 large onion, finely diced

1 cucumber, cut into ½ in (1 cm) cubes

small bunch of flat leaf parsley, finely chopped

freshly squeezed juice of 1 lemon

fine salt

Known as *çoban salata* in Turkish, this salad goes well with every type of kebab, since it is so refreshing and zingy. Sometimes when we're short on time we will just make some lamb shish and stuff them into pita bread with this salad—a perfect mid-week meal.

Put all the ingredients in a bowl, mix well, and season with salt.

CYPRUS POTATO SALAD WITH ROMAINE LETTUCE, HERBS, SCALLIONS, LEMON & OLIVE OIL

SERVES 6–8

8 Cyprus potatoes, scrubbed but not peeled

4 leaves Romaine lettuce, shredded

5 scallions, thinly sliced

small bunch of flat leaf parsley, chopped (a little stalk is good)

small bunch of cilantro, chopped, with stalks

small bunch of mint, leaves only, shredded

freshly squeezed juice of 2 lemons

scant ½ cup (100 ml) extra-virgin olive oil

flaky sea salt and freshly ground black pepper

Cyprus potatoes are some of the best in the world due to the incredible red soil they are grown in. They have a great flavor and a waxy consistency that works especially well for potato salads, so I would recommend trying to hunt them down for this recipe. If you can't find them, use another variety of waxy potato.

Put the whole potatoes into a large pan of cold salted water. Bring to a gentle simmer over medium heat. Cook until just tender—about 30 minutes, depending on size. Once cooked, drain and leave to cool. Peel the potatoes and cut them into ¾ in (2 cm) cubes. Mix all the ingredients together and season with salt and pepper.

SEAFOOD

TARAMA WITH FRIED MUSSELS & MINT OIL

In Istanbul there are lots of street vendors selling little skewers of battered fried mussels served with *tarator*, a sauce made with walnuts. Proper *tarama*, as opposed to the neon pink stuff sold in supermarkets, is a thing of real beauty. I would recommend making it even if you don't have time to make the whole dish. It's wonderful served with warm flatbread, or even chargrilled toast.

First make the tarama: start by peeling off and discarding the skin from the cod roe. Put the roe in a small blender with the garlic, half the lemon juice, the soaked bread, and the water. Blend until smooth. With the machine running, gradually add both the oils. (This process can also be done with a hand-held electric mixer.) If the mixture gets too stiff, add a little warm water to bring it to the right consistency, then continue to add the oils. Taste to check the seasoning; add a little flaky salt if needed and more lemon juice if you wish. Set aside in the refrigerator.

Heat a large pan over high heat. When the pan is very hot, add the mussels and water (or beer) and cover with a lid. Cook the mussels for a few minutes, or until all the shells have opened. Discard any unopened shells.

Drain the mussels (reserve the liquid if you like, to make a lovely sauce for another fish dish) and leave them to cool. Once cool enough to handle, pick all the meat out and reserve it.

To make the batter, whisk the egg white to fairly stiff peaks. In another bowl, gradually whisk the beer into the flour to form a smooth batter. Fold in the egg whites and nigella seeds, and season with a little fine salt.

Heat the oil in a deep-fryer to 350°F (180°C). Alternatively, place a deep frying pan over high heat and add a ¾ in (2 cm) depth of sunflower oil. When it is hot enough, a small cube of bread added to the oil should sizzle immediately.

Dust the mussels in the all-purpose flour, then place in the batter. (You can thread the mussels on skewers to make them a little easier to cook, if you like.) Using a slotted spoon, lift them out one at a time and lower them carefully into the hot oil. Fry for about 1 minute, or until golden brown all over. Remove and drain on paper towels, and season with fine salt.

To serve, spoon some tarama onto a plate and place a few mussels on top. Drizzle with mint oil and sprinkle with the scallion.

SERVES 2–4

1 lb 2 oz (500 g) mussels, cleaned and de-bearded

about 3 tablespoons water or beer

sunflower oil, for frying

fine salt

all-purpose flour, for dusting

1 quantity Mint Oil (see page 154), for drizzling

2 scallions, finely sliced on the diagonal, to garnish

FOR THE TARAMA

2 oz (55 g) smoked cod roe, soaked in cold water for 2 hours

½ garlic clove

freshly squeezed juice of 1 lemon

½ slice white bread, crusts removed, soaked in water

2 tablespoons water

3½ tablespoons sunflower oil

1¾ tablespoons olive oil

flaky sea salt

FOR THE BATTER

1 large egg white

1¼ cups (300 ml) cold beer or sparkling water

scant 1½ cups (6 oz/175 g) self-rising flour

2½ teaspoons nigella seeds

SEAFOOD VERMICELLI WITH MUSSELS, HAKE & SHRIMP

12 shell-on raw shrimp

1¼ cups (300 ml) fish stock

⅔ cup (150 ml) extra-virgin olive oil

1 onion, diced

1 carrot, diced

2 celery sticks, diced

3 sprigs of thyme, leaves only

½ teaspoon finely grated nutmeg

1 teaspoon ground coriander

1–2 red chilies, sliced and seeds retained

1 teaspoon tomato paste

1 tablespoon sweet pepper paste (tatlı biber salçası)

4 garlic cloves, finely grated

½ cup (120 ml) red wine

scant ½ cup (100 g) puréed tomatoes

2¼ cups (7 oz/200 g) broken vermicelli pieces

1 lb 2 oz (500 g) mussels, cleaned and de-bearded

11 oz (315 g) hake fillet (or any white fish), cleaned and cut into 1½ in (4 cm) cubes

small bunch of flat leaf parsley, finely shredded

1 lemon, cut into wedges

flaky sea salt and freshly ground black pepper

Shredded vermicelli is called şehriye in Turkish. It is often cooked with rice for an extra nutty flavor, or in soups. Here I have made it into a complete dish, taking inspiration from the Spanish dish fideuà. You can mix and match whichever fish and shellfish you like, and even include some chicken or rabbit if you want. If you have time, do make your own fish stock— this gives depth to the dish, and it needs to be packed full of flavor.

Start by peeling the shrimp: you can leave the heads on if you wish. Mix the shells with the fish stock in a pan and bring to a gentle simmer for 15 minutes. Remove from the heat and leave to infuse.

———

Heat the oil in a large pan over a medium heat, add the onion, carrot, celery, and thyme and cook gently for about 20 minutes, or until very soft. Add the spices, chili, tomato paste, sweet pepper paste, and garlic and continue to cook for 5 minutes.

———

Increase the heat to high and add the red wine. Bubble to reduce by half, then add the puréed tomatoes and strain in the fish stock. Season with salt and pepper. Turn down to a gentle simmer and cook for 15 minutes.

———

Now stir in the vermicelli, mussels, hake, and shrimp. Cover with a lid and cook for about 5 minutes, or until the vermicelli is soft, the mussels have opened (discard any that haven't), the shrimp have turned pink, and the hake is opaque. Taste to check the seasoning, sprinkle with the parsley, and serve with lemon wedges.

CUTTLEFISH WITH BAHARAT, PEAS & SEA BEANS

Just after finishing college, a few of my friends and I went to Spain for a celebratory trip to visit a friend whose family owns a campsite. One evening, my friend's mom cooked us a selection of dishes, including *sepia*, or cuttlefish. At the time I had no idea what *sepia* was and she couldn't really explain it to me, but she did say that she had cooked it with peas and cinnamon. It was so yummy that I made a note of it. It wasn't until years and years later that I referred back to that notebook and, knowing more about food at this point, realized it was cuttlefish. So here is my version of that dish.

Cut open the cuttlefish and score the inside in a cross-hatch pattern. Slice it into irregular diamond shapes about 1½ in (4 cm) wide. Pat the cuttlefish dry with paper towels and keep in the refrigerator until needed.

———

Heat the measured olive oil in a small saucepan and add the onion. Cook over medium heat until light golden brown. Remove from the heat and add the baharat.

———

Heat a large frying pan and add 1 tablespoon olive oil. Add the cuttlefish and let it fry for at least 1 minute before moving it; you want the edges to caramelize. After that, move the fish around a little in the pan and cook for 1 more minute. Now add the cooked onion, peas, and sea beans and cook for 1 more minute, or until the sea beans have just wilted. Remove the pan from the heat, add the lemon juice, season with salt and pepper, and add a little more olive oil to make a dressing in the pan. Finally, stir in the herbs and serve.

SERVES 4

2 cuttlefish with tentacles, cleaned

scant ½ cup (100 ml) extra-virgin olive oil, plus a little extra for frying

1 onion, diced

2 tablespoons baharat (see page 193; also available in Turkish supermarkets)

1 cup (4½ oz/125 g) peas, fresh or frozen

3½ oz (100 g) sea beans (also called samphire greens or sea asparagus)

freshly squeezed juice of 1 lemon

3 sprigs of mint, leaves only, thinly sliced

4 sprigs of parsley, finely chopped

flaky sea salt and freshly ground black pepper

FRIED RED MULLET, PICKLED APRICOTS & CAPER LEAVES

⅓ cup (1¾ oz/50 g) capers, lightly rinsed, or caper leaves

1 onion, cut into large cubes

small bunch of flat leaf parsley, leaves only

small bunch of cilantro, leaves only

small bunch of purslane, roughly chopped

3½ tablespoons extra-virgin olive oil, plus extra for frying

2 tablespoons red wine vinegar

4 red mullet, scaled and gutted, filleted if you prefer

1 teaspoon fine salt

¾ cup (3½ oz/100 g) all-purpose flour

flaky sea salt and freshly ground black pepper

FOR THE PICKLED APRICOTS

1¼ cups (300 ml) water

½ cup (3½ oz/100 g) sugar

1 tablespoon coriander seeds, lightly toasted and crushed

⅔ cup (150 ml) cider vinegar

12 dried apricots, preferably unsulphured, halved

This dish pays homage to my *nene*'s fried fish. While I was growing up, we would visit my grandparents in Cyprus every summer, and one of the first things Nene (Grandma) would cook is fried fish with a big bowl of salad. Dede (Grandpa) would go to the nearest town to pick up a bag of mixed little fish, a trip that I think took almost four hours by the time he had stopped off for a coffee and put the world to rights with his friends (also bearing in mind that his favored mode of transport was his tractor).

First make the pickled apricots: put the water in a pan with the sugar, coriander seeds, and vinegar. Bring it to a boil and add the apricots. Reduce the heat to a simmer and cook gently for 5 minutes. Using a slotted spoon, lift out the apricots and set aside in a bowl. Turn the heat back up to reduce the liquid to a light syrup. Once it is the right consistency, pour it over the apricots and leave to cool.

Add the capers, onion, parsley, cilantro, purslane, olive oil, and vinegar to the cooled apricots, along with a little of their syrup. Season with salt and pepper.

Season the fish with the fine salt and leave for about 10 minutes. Heat a ¾ in (2 cm) depth of oil in a large frying pan over medium heat. Place the fish in the flour and coat well, rubbing the flour mixture thoroughly into the fish.

Lower the fish carefully into the hot oil and fry until the underside is golden—about 3 minutes. Turn the fish over and do the same on the other side. Drain on paper towels and season with a little more fine salt. Serve with a pile of the apricot salad plus an extra drizzle of the apricot syrup and olive oil.

PISTACHIO-CRUSTED COD WITH PRESERVED LEMON BUTTER SAUCE

SERVES 4

4 cod fillets (from a sustainable source), about 6 oz (175 g) each, skinned and pin-boned

FOR THE PISTACHIO CRUST

¾ cup (3½ oz/100 g) shelled pistachios,

¼ cup (½ oz/15 g) fresh breadcrumbs

5 tablespoons (2½ oz/70 g) unsalted butter, softened

FOR THE PRESERVED LEMON SAUCE

1 whole preserved lemon (see page 201)

⅔ cup (150 ml) heavy cream

5½ tablespoons (2¾ oz/75 g) cold unsalted butter, diced

small bunch of chives, thinly sliced

Most people think of nuts as a snack, or associate them with desserts. However, I love using them in savory recipes too, especially pistachios—the lovely nutty flavor compliments all sorts of dishes. Some of the best pistachios in the world come from Gaziantep in Turkey, so if you see them, be sure to buy them.

First make the pistachio crust: put all the ingredients in a food processor and blend to a coarse paste. Spread a little of the paste over each cod fillet to make a layer about ¼ in (5 mm) thick, then set aside in the refrigerator.

———

Preheat the oven to 425°F (220°C). To make the sauce, scoop the flesh out of the preserved lemon and put the flesh in a small saucepan with the cream. Bring to a boil, then turn down to a simmer, and reduce by one-third.

———

Finely dice the preserved lemon skin. Once the cream has reduced, remove the pan from the heat and whisk in the butter a cube at a time. Strain through a fine sieve and add the diced lemon skin. Cover with plastic wrap and keep warm until needed.

———

Bake the cod in the oven for 7–9 minutes, or until just firm to touch and lightly colored on top. Stir the chives into the preserved lemon sauce and serve with the fish.

SEA BASS WITH CARAMELIZED SHALLOT PURÉE & POMEGRANATE DRESSING

Sea bass is one of the most popular fish in Turkey and Cyprus, usually served simply charcoal-grilled with a wedge of lemon. The thing I love about eating fish over there is that it is so seasonal, which not only protects the local species from being overfished but also ensures you get to eat them at their best. Other popular fish in the eastern Mediterranean are sea bream, turbot, grouper, blue fish, and red mullet, and can be used instead of sea bass.

Preheat the oven to 400°F (210°C).

First make the purée: melt the butter in a medium saucepan and add the shallots. Cook over low heat until golden brown—this can take up to 30 minutes.

Meanwhile, heat the oil in an ovenproof frying pan. Add the banana shallots, cut-side down. When they start to turn golden-brown, put the pan in the oven and roast the shallots for about 15 minutes.

While the shallots for the purée are still hot, put them in a blender with the cream and blend until smooth. Season with salt and pepper.

To make the dressing, combine all the ingredients in a bowl and whisk together.

To cook the fish, heat a drizzle of oil in a non-stick frying pan over medium-high heat. Season the sea bass, place in the pan skin-side down, and cook gently until the skin is golden brown and crisp (this should take no more than a few minutes). Turn it over and cook the flesh side for 30–60 seconds, then take it out of the pan immediately so that it doesn't overcook.

To serve, reheat the purée and put a spoonful on each serving plate. Place the fish on top, skin-side up, and spoon over the pomegranate dressing. Add the roasted shallots. Stir the pomegranate dressing, since it will have separated, then dot it around the plates and serve.

SERVES 4

sunflower oil, for frying

2 banana shallots, unpeeled and halved lengthways

4 sea bass fillets, about 4⅓ oz (125 g) each, scaled and pin-boned

fine salt and freshly ground pepper

FOR THE CARAMELIZED SHALLOT PURÉE

2½ tablespoons (1¼ oz/35 g) unsalted butter

6 shallots, sliced

3½ tablespoons heavy cream

FOR THE POMEGRANATE DRESSING

3 tablespoons pomegranate seeds

3 tablespoons pomegranate molasses

1 banana shallot, finely chopped

6 tablespoons (90 ml) extra-virgin olive oil

1 small garlic clove, finely grated

1 teaspoon thyme leaves

PAN-FRIED MACKEREL, BLACK OLIVE CROUTE & TOMATO-POMEGRANATE SALAD

SERVES 4

sunflower oil, for frying

4 mackerel fillets, pin-boned

1 tablespoon ground fennel

2 tablespoons Aleppo pepper flakes (pul biber)

2 tablespoons black olive paste (available in Turkish supermarkets) or use tapenade instead

salt

FOR THE CROUTES

4 white baguette slices, cut diagonally, ½ in (1 cm) thick

olive oil, for drizzling

flaky sea salt

FOR THE SALAD

2 tomatoes, peeled and sliced

1 red onion, thinly sliced

2 long green Turkish peppers (Charleston peppers; use ordinary peppers if you can't find them), sliced

small bunch of flat leaf parsley, finely shredded

¼ cup (60 ml) extra-virgin olive oil

2 tablespoons pomegranate molasses

freshly ground black pepper

All along the Galata Bridge in Istanbul you will find small vendors, mostly on boats, selling grilled mackerel sandwiches called *balik ekmek*. They are utterly delicious. This is my slightly pimped-up version, but instead of making the croutes you could use a good crusty baguette.

Preheat the oven to 375°F (190°C).

First make the croutes. Drizzle a little olive oil on the slices of bread, sprinkle with salt, and put them on a baking tray. Bake for about 10 minutes, or until lightly golden and crisp.

Make the salad. Mix the tomatoes, red onion, peppers, parsley, olive oil, and pomegranate molasses with a little salt and pepper.

Heat a little sunflower oil in a large frying pan over medium-high heat. Season the mackerel on the flesh side with salt, ground fennel, and pepper flakes, pressing the seasoning in. Put the fish, skin-side down, in the hot frying pan and cook for about 2 minutes, or until the skin is golden and crisp. Turn it over and cook for 1 more minute, or until just cooked through.

To serve, spread some black olive paste over the croute, add some tomato salad, and place the mackerel on top.

MONKFISH, CITRUS, URFA CHILI DRESSING & CILANTRO

While I was researching food from the Byzantine era as a link between Turkey and Italy, I found a connection in the use of spices and *garum* (fish sauce). So I created a black pepper dressing, which later turned into an Urfa chili dressing. Any charcoal-grilled fish would work very well here.

Heat a barbecue until the coals turn grey. Alternatively, preheat the oven to 425°F (220°C).

First make the caramel: put the sugar in a heavy-based saucepan over high heat. Watch until it turns deep brown, carefully tilting the pan to swirl the sugar around. As soon as the caramel reaches the right color, carefully add the orange juice, standing well back. The caramel will seize up, so keep stirring into the edge of the pan to release it. The mixture will all come together and reduce as you cook it; you want a syrupy consistency. To test this, you can drizzle a little onto a plate and place it in the refrigerator (once cooled, it should hold its own shape without running too much). Finish it with a little squeeze of lemon juice. Set aside at room temperature.

Whisk together all the ingredients for the Urfa chili dressing, and set aside at room temperature.

Pat the monkfish dry with paper towels. Coat it in olive oil and season with salt. Place directly on the very hot barbecue rack. Cook for 4–5 minutes, then turn it over and cook for another 4–5 minutes; you want caramelized grill marks and for the fish to feel firm to the touch. Alternatively, place the monkfish in a large roasting pan and roast in the oven for 6–8 minutes on each side. Remove from the heat, add a drizzle of olive oil and a squeeze of lemon juice, then leave to rest for 10 minutes.

To serve, quickly flash the monkfish on the barbecue or in the oven to reheat. Put it on a serving plate and drizzle the blood orange caramel around it. Add a good helping of Urfa chili dressing, orange segments, and cilantro and serve straight away.

SERVES 4

- 1 monkfish tail (about 2 lb 4 oz/1 kg), trimmed and cleaned
- 2 tablespoons olive oil, plus a little extra
- 1 blood orange or ordinary orange, peeled and segmented
- small bunch of cilantro, leaves only, but with a little stalk
- squeeze of lemon juice
- flaky or fine sea salt

FOR THE BLOOD ORANGE CARAMEL

- ¼ cup (1¾ oz/50 g) sugar
- 2 blood oranges or ordinary oranges, juiced
- squeeze of lemon juice

FOR THE URFA CHILI DRESSING

- 3½ tablespoons Urfa red pepper flakes (isot biber)
- 3½ tablespoons fish sauce
- 2 tablespoons honey
- 2 tablespoons soy sauce
- 2 teaspoons ground cumin
- 2 teaspoons ground coriander
- ½ cup (120 ml) extra-virgin olive oil
- freshly squeezed juice of ½ lemon

OKLAVA AT HOME:
DINNER PARTY BY LAURA CHRISTIE

Dinner parties are the perfect excuse to try some of the more complex recipes in this book—see right for a suggested menu. Preparing these dishes may at times keep you away from your guests, but their amazed queries of "How did you make this?" will make it all worthwhile. We recommend serving these dishes on large sharing platters in the middle of the table.

Turkish wine is the obvious accompaniment to Turkish food. My white of choice would be Paşaeli Yapincak, which spends time in oak but still retains a ripe citrus note with touches of stone fruit and orange zest. It's enjoyable alone but fantastic with food, since the complexity added by the oak gives it enough backbone to stand up to the punchy flavors of Turkish cooking.

I first came across this wine on a trip to Istanbul with Selin. On our last night, we took a slightly hairy cab ride followed by a private water taxi to reach a fish restaurant on the very edge of the Bosporus. I wanted to try the Yapincak grape (pronounced "yap-in-jack"). The wine we drank was from a winemaker I had not previously come across but, carried away by the food and spectacular view, I forgot to make a note of the name. However, I did remember the distinctive label with its images of fish. Fast forward several weeks and I spotted the wine at a tasting in London. Accompanying it was the winemaker, Seyit, who has since become a great supporter of Oklava. Paşaeli are committed to promoting indigenous varieties, and Yapincak is native to the Şarköy area in Thrace. Minimum intervention is used in the vineyards, and organic wine methods are used as far is as practical in a modern, medium-sized winery.

A remarkable red for a dinner party is the Arcadia Cabernet Franc. Perfect with the bolder and fuller flavors of Turkish cooking, this wine will be a real surprise to any Turkish wine sceptics. The Arcadia winery was founded over ten years ago by father and daughter Zeynep and Ozcan, possibly the most welcoming hosts in Turkey. Selin and I first visited Arcadia in the summer of 2015, and it is everything I have come to love about small-scale wine production—a family affair and a project of real passion. Great care is taken to look after the land, involve the community, and insist on careful production methods. The end products are amazing wines that reflect the beauty of their surroundings.

Cabernet Franc is an international grape, so the flavor profile of this wine, which includes plum, blackcurrant, and liquorice, and aromas like tobacco (from the year spent in French oak) will be familiar to many. Full-bodied with elegant tannins, it benefits from being decanted—or simply pour the wine into glasses and enjoy an aperitif while giving it a few minutes to open up.

DINNER PARTY MENU: FOR 6–8 PEOPLE

BAHARAT-SPICED BREAD WITH MEDJOOL DATE BUTTER (PAGES 46 & 186)

SOUR CHERRY PEARL BARLEY, CRISPY KALE, YOGURT, CHILI BUTTER & SHEEP'S CHEESE (PAGE 157)

ROMAINE LETTUCE SALAD WITH CANDIED WALNUTS & FETA DRESSING (PAGE 18)

CHILI-ROASTED CAULIFLOWER (PAGE 136)

RICOTTA DUMPLINGS WITH YOGURT SAUCE, CHILI BUTTER & PINE NUTS (PAGE 154)

SEA BASS WITH CARAMELIZED SHALLOT PURÉE & POMEGRANATE DRESSING (PAGE 126)

ÇEMEN-BRAISED SHORT RIBS WITH BROWN BUTTER BREAD SAUCE (PAGE 86)

CRISPY POMEGRANATE-GLAZED LAMB WITH YOGURT (PAGE 96)

SPICED RICE PUDDING BRÛLÉE, PISTACHIOS, CARAMELIZED PINEAPPLE, RUM JELLO, LYCHEES & LIME (PAGE 207)

TURKISH COFFEE (PAGE 172)

OKLAVA AT HOME:
DATE NIGHT BY LAURA CHRISTIE

**DATE NIGHT MENU:
DINNER FOR TWO**

BAHARAT-SPICED BREAD
WITH MEDJOOL DATE
BUTTER (PAGES 46 & 186)

ZUCCHINI, FETA & MINT
FRITTERS WITH
WHIPPED FETA &
MUHAMMARA
(PAGES 24 & 190)

PISTACHIO-CRUSTED
COD WITH PRESERVED
LEMON BUTTER SAUCE
OR SPICED BRAISED
OXTAIL WITH SHALLOTS
(PAGES 125 OR 92)

BUTTERED FREEKEH
WITH CHICKPEAS, GREEN
OLIVES, CURRANTS &
PISTACHIOS (PAGE 159)

MUHALLEBI WITH
STRAWBERRY JELLO
OR CHOCOLATE, PRUNE
& CARDAMOM DELICE
(PAGES 220 OR 212)

For date night, keep things simple but impressive. Our Cypriot 75 cocktail (see page 180) makes an elegant start to any special evening: it is very simple to make if you have a lot of cooking to do, and the flavors are neither too sweet nor too bitter. It's also easy to top up if you decide to stick to the cocktail through the meal.

A favorite wine for date nights at the restaurant is Kalecik Karası, pronounced "kah-le-jik car-ah-su" (or KK, as we call it for short). Among the things we love about Turkish wines are the names of the grapes, and this one means "black from the small castle." Kalecik is a small village with a castle north-east of Ankara in Central Anatolia, and it's the home of this grape variety. Also located near Ankara is the producer of this wine, Vinkara, a sophisticated and modern winery with a passion for indigenous varieties. Most of the Turkish wine that makes it to export comes from the Aegean region, so getting some inland examples on the list has been fantastic.

Kalecik Karası typifies exactly what I want to serve at Oklava: wines that are recognizable to the palate but have their own unique twist. The slightly gamey and savory notes against a background of redcurrant and sweet spice in this light red remind me of a Gamay or Pinot Noir, but the red-rose color and slight candy on the nose are classically Turkish, making this an interesting and complex wine, perfect for a romantic evening in.

CHILI-ROASTED CAULIFLOWER

I created this dish after my first visit to Istanbul. I had brought back with me a hot sun-dried pepper paste and some pistachios from one of the incredible markets out there. At home one evening, I had a cauliflower, some parsley, and the pepper paste in my fridge—and so the chili-roasted cauliflower was born. I cooked it at my very first pop-up restaurant, where it became an instant hit, and it is now our top seller at Oklava.

Preheat the oven to 400°F (210°C) and line a baking tray with parchment paper. Cut the cauliflower into 4–6 even wedges depending on its size, keeping a little of the stalk on to hold the wedges. Rinse under cold water and pat dry with paper towels.

Mix the two pepper pastes with the olive oil and a little salt. Rub the mixture all over the cauliflower wedges (you might want to wear gloves to do this) and put them on the prepared baking tray. Bake for 10–13 minutes, or until just tender. I like to make sure the cauliflower still has a good bite to it. Set aside.

Drain the red onions, pat dry with paper towels, and set aside.

Heat a dry non-stick frying pan on the stovetop. Once hot, add the cauliflower wedges and cook for a minute or so on each side, or until slightly charred.

To serve, put the wedges on a large plate and top with the parsley, red onion, and pistachios. Drizzle with plenty of the sumac dressing and an extra sprinkling of sumac before serving.

SERVES 4–6

1 cauliflower (keep the green leaves on if they are nice)

2 heaped tablespoons Turkish hot pepper paste (açi biber salçasi)

4 heaped tablespoons Turkish sweet pepper paste (tatli biber salçasi)

3½ tablespoons extra-virgin olive oil

½ red onion, sliced as thinly as possible and soaked in ice water

1 large handful flat leaf parsley leaves

⅓ cup (1½ oz/40 g) pistachio nuts, toasted and roughly chopped

1 quantity Sumac Dressing (see page 194)

1 teaspoon sumac

flaky sea salt

SPICY RED LENTIL KÖFTES WITH LETTUCE, SCALLIONS & LEMON

We sometimes had these as a tasty light meal on a hot summer day when I was growing up. They can also be made with raw ground lamb instead of red lentils; that version is called *cig köfte*. Expert makers knead these for ages by hand, and street vendors all around Turkey used to sell raw lamb *köfte*, ready to be cooked at home. These lentil *köftes* are great for any time of the week, even Sunday brunch.

Heat the olive oil in a pan over medium heat, add the onions, and cook for about 10 minutes, or until tender and translucent. Add the cumin, paprika, and hot pepper paste and cook for 1 more minute. Add the lentils and stir well. Cover with enough cold water to reach ¾ in (2 cm) above the lentils. Bring to a boil, reduce the heat to low, and cook for about 20 minutes, or until nearly all the water has evaporated and the lentils are cooked through. You might need to add a little more water. Turn the heat off and add the bulgur. Stir well, cover the pan with plastic wrap, and leave to stand for 30 minutes. Slice 3 of the scallions diagonally and place them in iced water.

———

Remove the plastic wrap from the lentil mixture and transfer to a large bowl. Let it cool a little before seasoning with salt. Finely slice the remaining scallions and add to the lentils, along with the chopped parsley. Knead the mixture well for 10 minutes, or put it in a stand mixer and beat with the paddle attachment until the mixture forms a ball.

———

Now divide the mixture into 25–30 equal size pieces and shape into sausages or balls, depending on how big you would like them to be. Arrange the lettuce leaves on a serving platter with the sliced scallions, the sprigs of parsley, and the lemon wedges. To eat them, take a lettuce leaf and place a köfte inside, then top with scallions, parsley, and a good squeeze of lemon.

MAKES 25–30

scant 1 cup (200 ml) extra-virgin olive oil

2 onions, finely chopped

1 heaped teaspoon ground cumin

1 heaped teaspoon sweet smoked paprika

2 tablespoons hot pepper paste (açi biber salçasi)

2⅓ cups (1 lb/450 g) red lentils, rinsed with cold water

1⅔ cups (9¾ oz/275 g) fine bulgur

1½ bunches of scallions, thinly sliced

bunch of flat leaf parsley, finely chopped (a little stalk it good), plus extra sprigs to serve

1 head of Romaine lettuce

2 lemons, cut into wedges

fine salt

SPICED CHICKPEAS, BUTTERED CABBAGE, POACHED DUCK EGG & TULUM CHEESE

This dish is perfect for lunch, or even brunch. Chickpeas take on all sorts of flavors and lots of spice really well, so if you like things hot, add more Urfa chili. For some extra texture you could add Çemen Crumbs too (see page 39).

Heat the olive oil in a pan over medium heat, add the onion, and cook gently for about 10 minutes, or until completely soft. Add the garlic, spices, and tomato paste and continue to cook for a few minutes. Add the chickpeas and red wine. Increase the heat to reduce the wine by half, then add about 3 tablespoons water and season with salt and pepper. Turn the heat right down and cook gently for 10 minutes.

———

Meanwhile, bring a small pan of water to a boil, add the vinegar, and lower the heat to a simmer. Crack the duck eggs into the water, then cook them to your liking; if you prefer them soft, you just want to set the white and the yolk should be soft when you touch it. (If you want to do these in advance, you can poach the eggs, then transfer them to iced water until needed. To serve, gently reheat them in a pan of water.)

———

While the eggs are cooking, melt the butter in a pan, add the cabbage leaves with a splash of water, cover, and cook for 2–3 minutes, or until wilted. Season with salt and pepper.

———

Stir some of the parsley through the chickpeas and divide them between 2 serving bowls. Scatter with the cabbage and top each serving with an egg. Scatter with the cheese and a little more parsley to serve.

SERVES 2

- scant ½ cup (100 ml) extra-virgin olive oil
- 1 onion, chopped
- 3 garlic cloves, finely grated
- 1 heaped teaspoon sweet smoked paprika
- 1 teaspoon ground fennel
- 2 tablespoons Urfa red pepper flakes (isot biber)
- 1 tablespoon tomato paste
- 14 oz (400 g) canned chickpeas, drained and rinsed
- ½ cup (120 ml) red wine
- 2 tablespoons white vinegar
- 2 duck eggs, the freshest you can find
- 1 teaspoon unsalted butter
- ¼ head of sweetheart cabbage, cored and leaves separated
- small bunch of flat leaf parsley, chopped (a little stalk is good)
- 4 tablespoons tulum cheese or any strong, crumbly cheese
- flaky sea salt and freshly ground black pepper

SLOW-COOKED WHITE BEANS WITH TOMATO, LEMON & OLIVE OIL

1 cup (250 ml) extra-virgin olive oil

2 carrots, diced

2 celery sticks, diced

2 onions, diced

1 bay leaf

2 sprigs of thyme, leaves only

3 garlic cloves, thinly sliced

2 cups (14 oz/400 g) dried white beans, such as cannellini, soaked overnight

½ small head of cabbage, finely shredded

3-4 large tomatoes, peeled and roughly diced

small bunch of flat leaf parsley, chopped (a little stalk is good)

1 sprig of tarragon, leaves only

1 sprig of marjoram or oregano, leaves only, chopped

finely grated zest of 1 lemon

flaky sea salt and freshly ground black pepper

The Turks love their beans and have all sorts of recipes for the different types, sometimes with meat and sometimes without. The key to this dish, traditionally made with a rich tomato sauce known as _kuru fasulye_, is to use the best ingredients you can get ahold of, since the flavors are very subtle. It is traditionally served with raw onion, bread, and parsley to mop up all the juices, a great mid-week meal. I especially like to cook this version in the summer months, since it tastes light and fresh because of the lemon zest.

Heat the oil in a large pan over low heat. Add the carrots, celery, onions, bay leaf, and thyme. Cover and cook gently for about 15 minutes, or until slightly softened. Add the garlic and continue to cook for 5 minutes.

———

Drain the beans, add to the pan, and pour in enough water to cover them by 2 in (5 cm). Gently cook for about 30 minutes, or until the beans are almost soft. You might need to add a bit more water if the pan starts to dry out.

———

Add the cabbage and tomatoes (there should be enough liquid to come halfway up the beans at this point; if there is too much, just spoon some out). Season with salt and pepper, cover, and cook for 5 minutes, or until the cabbage has wilted but still has a little bite.

———

Remove from the heat, check the seasoning, and add the parsley, tarragon, and marjoram. Serve in bowls and scatter with the lemon zest. A little extra olive oil, flaky sea salt, and parsley on top are always good too.

BARBECUED CORN WITH SUMAC, GARLIC, LEMON BUTTER & ZA'ATAR

In Cyprus people will set up a small barbecue just about anywhere, and you'll often see them selling freshly grilled corn-on-the cob in its husk. When I'm having a barbecue at home, I nearly always grill corn as one of the courses. I just love it, especially experimenting with all the different flavors it can take. I like to open up the pantry and see what jumps out at me.

SERVES 4

4 ears of corn, with husks

4 tablespoons unsalted butter, softened

1 tablespoon sumac

finely grated zest of 1 lemon

2 garlic cloves, finely grated

1 teaspoon flaky sea salt

2 tablespoons za'atar

4 sprigs of cilantro, mostly leaves with a little stalk

1 lime, cut into wedges

Heat a barbecue until the coals turn grey. Place the corn straight onto the rack and leave to blister and blacken slightly, turning them over.

———

Meanwhile, combine the butter, sumac, lemon, garlic, and salt in a bowl and mix well. You can make the butter ahead of time, if you like: just place it on a piece of plastic wrap, roll it into a sausage shape, and keep refrigerated until needed.

———

Once the corn is cooked to your liking, remove it from the grill, leave to cool just a little, and peel back the husks. Smear on the butter and sprinkle with za'atar. Garnish with cilantro and serve with wedges of lime.

BAKED LAMB-FAT POTATOES, FRIED DUCK EGG, GRILLED HELLIM & SHERRY VINEGAR CARAMEL

As a quick and easy dinner, Mom would sometimes sauté a pile of diced potatoes, then crack an egg onto it, or add some diced lamb with caramelized onion and parsley. It was one of my favorite meals. This is my rather more complex version of that dish, which captures the flavors of a good lamb roast with potatoes. Leftover fat from roast lamb is perfect here, or ask your butcher for lamb suet.

If using lamb suet, place it in a pan over a low heat, cook gently to draw out the fat, then strain through a sieve before using. Heat half the lamb fat or suet in a large pan over medium heat. Add the lamb breast, onions, and both types of peppers and cook for 45–60 minutes, or until completely softened. Season with fine salt. Once cooked, drain the lamb, adding the fat to the remaining lamb fat or suet and keep it warm.

———

Preheat the oven to 375°F (190°C) and line a deep baking tray (about 8 x 12 in/ 20 x 30 cm) with parchment paper. Cut the potatoes into $^1/_{16}$–$^1/_8$ in (2–3 mm) slices, using a mandoline if you have one. Coat the slices in the lamb fat in a heatproof bowl. If they get stuck together, hold the bowl over low heat or place briefly in the oven to melt the fat again.

———

Place 3 layers of potatoes in the bottom of the prepared tray, overlapping them a little and seasoning with salt. Add a thin layer of the lamb mixture, followed by another 2 layers of potatoes and seasoning. Keep

repeating this process until all the potatoes and lamb mixture are used up. Try to finish with 3 layers of potatoes on the top. Reserve any leftover fat.

———

Put a sheet of parchment paper directly on top of the potatoes and push them down so they are evenly spread out in the tray and into the corners. Cover with foil and bake for about 45–60 minutes, until the potatoes are soft (check by poking a skewer or knife into the center).

———

Once cooked, remove from the oven and leave to rest for 40 minutes. Place another tray and a weight on top to press it down, then chill the gratin for at least 3 hours, or overnight.

———

Preheat the oven to 400°F (200°C). To release the gratin, you'll need to warm the tray, either by using a blowtorch or running it over a low heat. Turn it out and cut into 12 portions. Heat a frying pan with a little more lamb fat (or sunflower oil) and add the portions of gratin. Cook until crispy and golden on both sides. Transfer to a baking tray and put in the oven for 5 minutes to heat through.

———

Meanwhile, fry the duck eggs in more lamb fat or sunflower oil. In a separate frying pan, fry the slices of hellim in a little sunflower oil until golden brown on both sides. Serve the eggs on top of the hot gratin with a drizzle of sherry vinegar caramel, a slice of hellim, and a few parsley leaves to garnish.

SERVES 12

7–10½ oz (200–300 g) lamb fat or lamb suet, melted

9 oz (250 g) lamb breast, sliced into small pieces

1–2 onions, chopped

4 long green Turkish peppers (Charleston peppers; use ordinary peppers if you can't find them), sliced

4 hot Turkish peppers (sivri biber; use any hot chilies if you can't find them)

8 large white potatoes (we like to use the Cyprus variety)

sunflower oil, for frying (optional)

12 duck eggs

1 x 9 oz (250 g) block hellim (halloumi), sliced into 6

1 quantity Sherry Vinegar Caramel (see page 195)

flat leaf parsley leaves, to garnish

fine salt

CRISPY FRIED SCALLIONS, CHEESE SAUCE & ÇEMEN CRUMBS

A few years ago I discovered *calçots*, the delicious scallions from Catalonia in Spain. I tried preparing them in the traditional way, which is to blacken them, peel off the outer layer, and eat them with romesco sauce. As delicious as this was, I had an urge to fry them in spiced flour. This is a great, indulgent dish by itself, or you could serve it as a garnish with grilled steak, or even top a *pide* with them. If you can find *calçots*, I would recommend using them.

Mix the flour with the spices and measured salt, and set aside.

———

Slice the onions diagonally into ½ in (1 cm) slices. Whisk the milk and yogurt together in a bowl. Add the onions and leave to soak for about 30 minutes.

———

Heat the oil in a deep-fryer to 350°F (180°C). Alternatively, half-fill a deep frying pan with oil and set over high heat. When hot enough, a small cube of bread added to the oil should sizzle immediately.

———

Take a handful of the scallions, shake off the excess milk mixture, and coat them in the flour. Transfer to a sieve and shake off the excess flour, then add them carefully to the hot oil and fry for about 2 minutes, or until golden brown. Remove and drain on paper towels to soak up the excess oil and season with fine salt.

———

To serve, put the cheese sauce in a large bowl or several smaller bowls and top with a mound of fried scallions and a generous sprinkling of çemen crumbs.

SERVES 4–6

1⅔ cups (7 oz/200 g) all-purpose flour

1 heaped tablespoon sweet smoked paprika

1 heaped tablespoon ground coriander

1 heaped tablespoon ground cumin

1 heaped tablespoon ground fennel

1 tablespoon fine salt, plus extra to season

2 bunches of scallions or calçots, outer layers removed

1¼ cups (300 ml) milk

scant ½ cup (100 ml) Turkish or Greek yogurt

sunflower oil, for frying

1 quantity Cheese Sauce (see pages 56 and 65)

1 quantity Çemen Crumbs (see page 39)

SPICED RICE, APRICOT, ALMOND & FILO PIE

SERVES 6

11 tablespoons (5½ oz/150 g) unsalted butter

3½ tablespoons extra-virgin olive oil

1 onion, diced

3 garlic cloves, finely grated

1 teaspoon ground cumin

1 tablespoon fennel seeds, toasted and ground

1 tablespoon ground coriander

1 teaspoon freshly grated nutmeg

1 cup (6½ oz/185 g) long-grain rice, rinsed

⅔ cup (3 oz/85 g) dried apricots (preferably unsulphured), diced

¾ cup (3½ oz/100 g) whole blanched almonds, toasted and roughly chopped

1½ cups (350 ml) boiling water

2 large sheets of yufka, or 6 sheets filo pastry

flaky sea salt and freshly ground black pepper

Known as *perde pilav* in Turkish, this is a very traditional recipe, for which people would usually make their own dough and roll it out very thinly. Here I have tried to make it a little easier by using filo pastry (or the Turkish version, *yufka*, if you can find it, which is available in most Turkish supermarkets). If you like, you can use different spices, nuts, and fruit than those listed, and even mix in a little shredded chicken or duck.

Melt 7 tablespoons (3½ oz/100 g) of the butter with the olive oil in a large pan over medium heat. Add the onion and cook gently for 10 minutes, or until golden. Add the garlic and all the spices and continue to cook for 5 minutes over low heat. Now add the rice and season with salt and pepper, stirring to ensure it is well coated. Add the apricots, almonds, and boiling water. Bring to a boil, then turn the heat down to its lowest setting, cover, and cook for 20 minutes, or until all the water has evaporated and the rice is cooked.

—

Remove the rice from the pan and spread it out on a tray to cool down completely. Preheat the oven to 425°F (220°C).

—

Melt the remaining butter and use some of it to lightly grease an 8 in (20 cm) round cake pan. If using yufka, drape the first sheet over the pan and press it down into the bottom and sides, allowing the excess to hang over the edge. Fill the pan with the rice mixture, pressing it out firmly and evenly. Fold the overhanging pastry over the filling and brush it with a little butter. Trim the second sheet so that it is just a little bigger than the pan. Place it on the top of the rice and, using a spoon, tuck in all the corners neatly. Brush the top with butter. If using filo, follow the same procedure, using 3 sheets to line the pan and 3 trimmed sheets on top, brushing each sheet with butter.

—

Bake for about 25 minutes, or until golden brown and crisp. Remove the pie from the oven and leave to rest for 5 minutes. Carefully turn it onto a plate and leave to rest for another 10 minutes. Slice into 6 portions to serve.

VEGETABLE DOLMAS

These are called *yalanci dolma* in Turkish: dolma refers to anything stuffed, and *yalanci* means "liar," since this version does not contain the usual meat. Mom is a complete pro at any sort of dolma, and is known in our circle for making the best. Throughout the summer she makes them using vine leaves, which she grows herself in the garden, and in the winter she moves on to different types of cabbage. This version, using cabbage leaves, is a good place to start, and once you have mastered it, you can move onto vine leaves, which are a little trickier to handle. You could also use the Artichoke Dolma filling (see page 84) to stuff cabbage or vine leaves.

Bring a large pan of water to a boil. Separate the cabbage leaves, making sure you keep them intact. As long as the leaf is big enough to roll into a cigar shape, it is usable.

In a large bowl, mix together the rice, onions, tomatoes, mint, oil, and lemon juice, then season with salt and pepper. Set aside.

Blanch the cabbage leaves in batches of 5 for about 1 minute, until they are just pliable. Remove and place on a large tray to cool.

To make the dolmas, take a large cabbage leaf and place a heaped tablespoon of the rice mixture in a line across the stalk end, as in the photo opposite. Do not go right to the edges. Working from the edge closest to you, roll up the leaf tightly to form a cigar shape. The sides will roll in naturally. Put the dolma in a large, wide-based pan with a lid.

Repeat the process until all the leaves are used up or you run out of mixture. As the leaves get smaller you will need less stuffing. It is very important to pack the dolmas in tight layers in the pan. It's fine to put them on top of one another, but do not go right to the top of the pan; you need to leave room for them to expand. Boil the kettle and pour over just enough hot water to cover the top layer of dolmas. Put an upside-down plate directly on top of the dolmas to hold them down. Set the pan over high heat; as soon as the water comes to the boil, reduce the heat to medium-low, put the lid on, and cook for 40–45 minutes, or until all the water has evaporated.

Once cooked, take the pan off the heat and remove the plate. Put a couple of pieces of paper towel on top of the dolmas and put the lid back on. Leave to stand for about 15-20 minutes before serving; I like them best served at room temperature.

SERVES 8–10

2 whole Savoy or green cabbages, stalks removed

2¾ cups (1 lb 2 oz/500 g) white long-grain rice, rinsed

2 onions, finely chopped

14 oz (400 g) canned plum tomatoes, chopped

2 tablespoons dried mint

½ cup (120 ml) extra-virgin olive oil

freshly squeezed juice of 2-3 lemons (we like our dolmas with a zing; use 2 if you don't)

flaky sea salt and freshly ground black pepper

RICOTTA DUMPLINGS WITH YOGURT SAUCE, CHILI BUTTER & PINE NUTS

These small pasta dumplings are called *pirohu* in Cyprus and *manti* in Turkey. My version takes a little time, but I believe it's totally worth the effort.

First make the dumpling dough: mix the flour and salt in a bowl. Keep mixing while you slowly pour in the water until a dough forms. Tip it onto a floured surface and knead for about 5 minutes, or until smooth. Cover with plastic wrap and rest in the refrigerator for at least 1 hour.

To make the mint oil, put the dried mint and olive oil in a small pan and heat gently for 5 minutes. Set aside to infuse.

To make the sauce, heat the olive oil in a pan, add the shallots, and cook gently until golden brown. Add the garlic and thyme and cook for a further few minutes. Now add the wine and simmer to reduce by half, then add the cream and reduce by one-third. Remove from the heat and whisk in the yogurt. Using a stick blender, blend the sauce until smooth and season with salt. Leave to cool and set aside in the refrigerator.

Preheat the oven to 400°F (210°C). Put the cabbage wedges on a baking tray, drizzle with a little olive oil, and season with salt. Bake for about 15 minutes, or until the edges are a little charred and the cabbage is tender but not overcooked. Set aside. Turn the oven down to 350°F (180°C).

Combine the ingredients for the filling and season to taste. Set aside.

To make the dumplings, cut the dough in half and cover 1 piece with a damp dish towel. Roll the other into a circle $1/16$–$1/8$ in (2–3 mm) thick.

Dot about 18 teaspoons of the ricotta mixture across one half of the pastry sheet, spaced evenly apart. Brush the other half of the circle lightly with water if it seems to be too dry to stick by itself. Fold over the circle and push down to seal the edges neatly around each pile of ricotta. Cut out each dumpling using a cup or pastry cutter. Place on a tray or plate heavily dusted with semolina. Repeat with the remaining dough and filling.

Bring a large pan of salted water to a boil. Melt the chili butter and keep it warm. Cut the stalks out of the cabbage quarters and put them in the oven to reheat. Gently reheat the yogurt sauce until it is just warm to the touch, then cover with a lid.

Working in batches, put the dumplings in the boiling water for 1–2 minutes. Transfer to a bowl with some of the cooking water to stop them sticking while you cook the rest. To serve, divide the cabbage and dumplings between 4 plates. Spoon on the warm yogurt sauce. Drizzle with some chili butter and mint oil. Finally, scatter with the pine nuts and thyme leaves.

MAKES ABOUT 36

1 small green cabbage, cut into 4 wedges

extra-virgin olive oil, for drizzling

semolina, for dusting

½ quantity Chili Butter (see page 186)

scant ½ cup (1¾ oz/50 g) pine nuts, lightly toasted

1 tablespoon thyme leaves

flaky fine salt

FOR THE DOUGH

2 cups (9 oz/250 g) all-purpose flour

½ teaspoon fine salt

scant 1 cup–1¼ cups (200–300 ml) cold water

FOR THE MINT OIL

1 teaspoon dried mint

¼ cup (60 ml) extra-virgin olive oil

FOR THE SAUCE

3½ tablespoons extra-virgin olive oil

3 banana shallots, chopped

3 garlic cloves, finely grated

1 sprig of thyme, leaves only

½ cup (120 ml) white wine

generous 2 cups (500 g) heavy cream

1¾ cups (400 ml) Turkish or Greek yogurt

FOR THE FILLING

2 cups (1 lb 2 oz/500 g) ricotta cheese

small bunch of flat leaf parsley, leaves only, chopped

small bunch of tarragon, leaves only, chopped

8 basil leaves, chopped

freshly ground black pepper

SOUR CHERRY PEARL BARLEY, CRISPY KALE, YOGURT, CHILI BUTTER & SHEEP'S CHEESE

SERVES 6–8

1 quantity Chili Butter (see page 186)

6 tablespoons Turkish or Greek yogurt

small bunch of mint, leaves only, shredded

small bunch of flat leaf parsley, leaves only, shredded

1 quantity Crispy Kale (see page 21)

¾ cup (2¼ oz/60 g) finely grated hard sheep's cheese, such as pecorino

FOR THE PEARL BARLEY

⅔ cup (150 ml) extra-virgin olive oil

6 banana shallots, thinly sliced

4 garlic cloves, thinly sliced

2½ cups (7 oz/200 g) dried sour cherries

1¼ cups (9 oz/250 g) pearl barley, rinsed with cold water

fine salt

I'm not sure how I came up with this dish, but I'm really glad I did. It's a big crowd pleaser, which I think is because it is quite unusual and you wouldn't expect pearl barley to be so full of flavor. It found its way onto the Oklava menu after a critic wrote a review of my residency at Carousel, describing it as a highlight of her year.

First prepare the pearl barley: heat the olive oil in a pan over very low heat, add the shallots, and cook very gently for 20 minutes, until soft but with no color. Add the garlic and continue to cook for 5 minutes. Add the sour cherries and pearl barley and stir to coat in the oil and shallots. Pour enough cold water into the pan to cover the barley by about ¾ in (2 cm). Gently cook over medium heat for about 30 minutes, or until just cooked through. Season with fine salt. Meanwhile, melt the chili butter and keep it warm.

Transfer the pearl barley mixture to a serving platter or individual plates. Put the yogurt in a squeezy bottle (if you have one) and drizzle it over the top. Add the herbs and a trickle of warm chili butter, top with the crispy kale, and sprinkle with the grated cheese.

BUTTERED FREEKEH WITH CHICKPEAS, GREEN OLIVES, CURRANTS & PISTACHIOS

SERVES 2–4

9 tablespoons (4½ oz/125 g) unsalted butter

3½ tablespoons extra-virgin olive oil

3 banana shallots, diced

3 garlic cloves, finely grated

1½ cups (9 oz/250 g) freekeh, rinsed under cold water

scant 1 cup (4½ oz/125 g) currants

1½ cups (7 oz/200 g) good-quality green olives, pitted and roughly chopped

3 cups (700 ml) water

14 oz (400 g) canned chickpeas, drained and rinsed

1¼ cups (5½ oz/150 g) shelled pistachios, toasted, and coarsely ground

small bunch of flat leaf parsley, chopped

small bunch of mint, leaves only, shredded

small bunch of chives, chopped

flaky sea salt and freshly ground black pepper

Freekeh is a brilliantly versatile grain with a rich, slightly smoky flavor that comes from roasting over an open fire. This is a great dish by itself, as part of a sharing mezze-style meal, or as an accompaniment to roasted meats or fish. We sometimes serve it with fried shrimp and a wedge of lemon.

Heat the butter and olive oil in a medium pan over medium heat. Add the shallots and cook gently for about 10 minutes, or until browned. Add the garlic and continue to cook for 2–3 minutes.

———

Now add the freekeh, currants, and olives and season with salt and pepper. Pour in the water, reduce the heat to low, and cover with a lid. Cook for about 30 minutes, stirring occasionally. Add a little extra water if it seems a bit dry. The freekeh should be just tender, but still with a little bite to it. Finally, add the chickpeas, pistachios, and herbs, check the seasoning, and serve.

OKLAVA AT HOME:
PERFECT PARTY FOOD BY LAURA CHRISTIE

At Oklava we believe that all special occasions should start with a glass of fizz. Our favorite is Kavaklidere Altın Köpük (literally "golden foam"), a fantastic wine from Turkey's oldest and probably best-known winery. The indigenous grape used is Emir, which means "lord," a name said to derive from the fact that Emir wines have occupied a place on the dinner tables of nobility as far back as Roman times.

Perfect as an aperitif, Altın Köpük is most easily comparable to Prosecco, and will be familiar in taste: predominantly green apple and white flower with a slight brioche note. This brioche note and a slight added complexity are due to the wine spending some time aging in contact with yeast. For this reason, it is a very interesting halfway house, production-wise, between Prosecco and wines made by the Champagne method.

For a Turkish take on the classic Bellini, mix Altın Köpük with a basic fruit purée or syrup—our favorites are bergamot, pomegranate, and rose. We recommend about 1½ tablespoons purée or syrup, depending on concentration, to ½ cup (120 ml) wine. This is a great option for a large group: you can pour the syrup or purée into glasses beforehand, ready to top up with bubbly just before serving. If you can't find Altın Köpük, any Prosecco-style sparkling wine will match well with these syrups or purées, and pair perfectly with Turkish flavors.

For a cocktail option, our Pomegranate & Sumac Martini (see page 176) is a great choice, since all the work can be done in advance and the mixture refrigerated until required. You could even skip the shaking-with-ice stage and add the lime to the prepared mixture for a speedy service, although shaking cocktails in front of guests is always a nice touch. If serving this drink pre-mixed, we recommend chilling the glasses in the freezer or with ice and water first.

The dishes listed on the right are perfect to be laid out buffet-style, or even passed around, leaving you to enjoy your evening without being tied to the stove.

PARTY MENU

FRIED BEEF KÖFTE WITH TOMATO RELISH (PAGES 89 & 189)

CUTTLEFISH WITH BAHARAT, PEAS & SEA BEANS (PAGE 120)

TOMATO, RAW ONION, PURSLANE, CRISP BREAD & MINT SALAD (PAGE 15)

SALAD OF ROMANO BEANS, CUCUMBER, FENNEL & KALE WITH A TOMATO DRESSING (PAGE 21)

FRIED VEGETABLES WITH GARLIC YOGURT & POMEGRANATE (PAGE 23)

VEGETABLE DOLMAS (PAGE 152)

SPICED BEEF & CHEESE SAUCE POĞAÇAS (PAGE 56)

SEMOLINA CUSTARD & FILO BÖREKS (PAGE 204)

DRINKS

HOMEMADE LIMONATA

As one famous food critic asked me in our opening weeks: is this just fancy lemonade? The answer is essentially yes. All over Istanbul you see street vendors selling fresh limonata, which is extremely refreshing and easy to make and store. It's a great addition to a barbecue or for any non-drinkers. Modifications to personal taste can easily be made with the addition of almost any other fruit. The amount of sugar can also be adjusted to taste.

Bring the sugar and water to a simmer in a saucepan and heat for about 5 minutes, or until the sugar dissolves and the mixture starts to thicken. Remove from the heat and allow to cool. Mix the sugar syrup with the lemon juice and store in the refrigerator until required.

———

To serve, fill a glass with ice and add 1½ tablespoons of the lemon mixture. Top up with still or sparkling water and serve with a slice of lemon or sprig of mint.

MAKES 4¼ CUPS
(1 LITER)

2½ cups (1 lb 2 oz/500 g) sugar

generous 2 cups (500 ml) water

generous 2 cups (500 ml) freshly squeezed lemon juice

lemon slices or mint sprigs, to serve

POMEGRANATE ICED TEA

We have always felt that it's a shame to have an interesting food and wine list but a dull soft drinks selection—an opinion Laura became more firm about on finding out she was expecting a baby a few months after Oklava opened. Pomegranate iced tea is very refreshing and simple to make, but has enough wow factor to impress guests. This recipe makes a big pitcher for sharing, but you could easily bottle and store it in the refrigerator for up to five days. It's easy to adapt the recipe—with green tea, for example, or any other kind of fruit.

Stir the sugar into the tea until dissolved, then stir in the pomegranate juice. Refrigerate until required.

———

To serve, fill the glasses with ice and pomegranate seeds, pour in the tea mixture, and serve immediately.

SERVES 6

2 tablespoons sugar

scant 1 cup (200 ml) light English breakfast tea, brewed for 1 minute

2½ cups (600 ml) pomegranate juice

pomegranate seeds

TRADITIONAL TURKISH ÇAY

Tea or *çay* (pronounced "chai") is deeply embedded in Turkish culture, and is an important element of hospitality. The Turkish element is the method used to brew the tea rather than its origin, although a huge amount of tea is produced domestically in Turkey. After World War I and the fall of the Ottoman Empire, importing coffee became hugely expensive, so the popularity of tea exploded. You will see it served everywhere in the traditional tulip-shaped glasses that have become as quintessentially Turkish as apple pie is American.

Tea is served without milk from a special teapot called a *çaydanlık*. This looks like two teapots stacked on top of each other: the bottom one is larger and is used to boil water, while the upper one is used to brew a very strong tea. Each serving of tea is then made by diluting liquid from the upper pot using water from the bottom pot according to the drinker's individual taste, and it is frequently served with sugar. As the tea is consumed, the upper pot is topped up with water from the bottom pot, and new water is added to the bottom pot to keep the tea going for several hours. Tea is drunk all year round and at every time of day—even during the very hot summers, when it is said to help cool you down. We were offered many glasses during our time in the markets of Istanbul as a friendly refresher during price negotiations, and it is also extremely popular served at home to welcome guests.

We use Özerlat tea in the restaurant, but any good Turkish supermarket will stock tea, or it is easily available online. If you are planning to be a regular drinker, electric *çaydanlıks* are easily available online and well worth the investment. If the tea is to be served with brunch, I would suggest using an ordinary teapot and a kettle. Use loose-leaf tea to brew a pot of strong tea for about 10 minutes, then pour it into glasses (or cups) and top up with hot water from the kettle. The color should be an amber-caramel tone, but try it beforehand and make the strength to your own taste. If you want to go the whole nine yards, the traditional tea glasses can be bought inexpensively from most Turkish supermarkets.

TURKISH APPLE TEA

SERVES 6

9 oz (250 g) apples

6 cups (1.4 liters) boiling water

1 tablespoon sugar

cinnamon or cloves (optional)

As well as traditional tea, *çay*, many other kinds of tea are available in Turkey, the most popular and widely known of which is apple tea. This recipe can be enjoyed hot in traditional glasses or cups, but is equally delicious cold. To serve it cold, simply allow to cool after brewing and store in the refrigerator. Variants on this mixture are easy: you could add different spices, other fruits, replace the sugar with honey—the list goes on. The type of apples you use is up to you. I prefer green apples for a fresher taste, but red would work equally well and are perhaps a better complement to any spices, if using.

Preheat the oven to 225°F (110°C). Core the apples, keeping the skin on, and cut them into roughly ¼ in (5 mm) cubes. Spread them out on a baking sheet, making sure no cubes overlap, and bake for 1 hour, or until completely dried, shaking the tray every 15 minutes. Dried apple can be stored in an airtight container for a few months.

Pour the boiling water into a pan with the apple cubes, sugar, and spices, if using. Stir until the sugar has dissolved, then simmer for about 10 minutes or slightly longer if you have added spices. To serve, strain the tea into heatproof glasses or cups.

AT-HOME AYRAN

Ayran is a very popular salted yogurt drink in Turkey, and you either love it or hate it. People who do love it really love it, and we are frequently drunk out of stock by a single table. *Ayran* was the soft drink of choice in Turkey until the introduction of modern carbonated drinks, and although it can be served at any time of day, I think it's particularly well suited to brunch. If serving it to a group, I recommend putting the salt on the table for people to add to their personal taste.

SERVES 6

3 cups (700 ml) plain yogurt
3 cups (700 ml) cold water
salt
dried mint, to garnish

Beat the yogurt in a bowl by hand or with an electric mixer, gradually adding the cold water until smooth. Add enough salt to season to your taste, but keep it light so that guests can add their own. Refrigerate until required.

To serve, fill the glasses with ice and pour in the yogurt mixture. Sprinkle the dried mint on top.

TURKISH COFFEE

Turkish coffee is essentially an unfiltered, short, black coffee, often sweetened with a little sugar, but variations of it exist all across the Middle East. Like tea, coffee is very important in terms of hospitality and tradition. For example, on visiting their fiancé's family home, suitors are traditionally subjected to salt in their coffee by their potential in-laws as a test of worthiness. The practice of reading the future in coffee grounds (a popular after-dinner activity) is also Turkish in origin. Many Oklava customers can be seen turning their cup upside down on the saucer, allowing the grounds to run down and settle. No formal training is required—just interpret the shapes you see forming.

If you are planning to serve Turkish coffee regularly, it might be worth investing in some proper Turkish coffee cups—these are slightly bigger than espresso cups and available online or in Turkish supermarkets. We use Özerlat coffee in the restaurant, produced by a family business that has been roasting coffee in north Cyprus for 100 years. Iley, the great-granddaughter of the company's founder, has become a great supporter of Oklava: our beautiful cups, handmade in Turkey, came via her.

To make Turkish coffee at home, you can use either a Turkish coffee pot, called a *cezve* (electric models, as well as traditional beaten copper pots, are available online), or a small milk pan. Before you start, you will need to find out if your guests would like sugar—for the uninitiated, we recommend half a teaspoon per cup—as adding sugar later disturbs the grounds and does not make for a great cup of Turkish coffee. If your guests have different sugar requirements, you will need to make their coffee in separate batches.

Add ¼ oz (7 g; about 1 rounded teaspoon) of finely ground coffee per cup and the required amount of sugar to the pan or *cezve*, then pour in a cup of water per person, using a cup you intend to serve in, and filling it right to the brim—espresso cups work well. Put the pan on medium heat and stir quickly and vigorously, then leave to brew until you start to see a foam form across the surface. This foam is extremely important: every good cup of Turkish coffee is covered with it. That is why we recommend making a maximum of 3 cups at a time—it is hard to get it right otherwise.

Once the foam starts to form, remove the coffee from the heat and pour a little into each cup. Return the remaining coffee to the heat and wait until it starts to gently bubble at the edges—do not let it boil. Remove from the heat as soon as you see those bubbles and top up the cups, pouring a little at a time into each one to spread the grounds and foam evenly. Serve the coffee on a saucer, without a teaspoon in order to prevent accidental stirring. The coffee will be hotter than your average espresso, so it is best to wait a few minutes for it to cool and the grounds to fully settle.

TURKISH BLOODY MARY

SERVES 6

2 tablespoons freshly
squeezed lemon juice

2 tablespoons Worcestershire
sauce

2 tablespoons olive brine

2 tablespoons turnip juice
(salgam)

1 teaspoon Tabasco sauce

2 tablespoons freshly grated
horseradish

2½ cups (600 ml) tomato
juice

1¼ cups (300 ml) good-quality
vodka

TO SERVE

1 lime

¼ cup (1 oz/25 g) sumac

6 breakfast radishes

nigella seeds, to sprinkle

salt and coarsely ground
black pepper

The idea for our Turkish Bloody Mary came about when we spotted a Turkish vodka on the price list of one of our suppliers. Having not even known that Turkey was a producer of vodka, we were keen to stock the spirit and, in keeping with everything else we do at Oklava, we decided to take the classic bloody Mary and make it Turkish. For the recipe below you can use any good-quality vodka; the tweaks to the recipe keep the Turkish feel.

Put the lemon juice, Worcestershire sauce, olive brine, turnip juice, and Tabasco in a large jug and give them a good stir. Once combined, add the fresh horseradish and tomato juice and stir again. Try the mixture at this point to ensure the spice level is to your taste; you can add more Tabasco as required.

———

Cut the lime into wedges and rub one around the top of each serving glass. Spread the sumac out on a shallow saucer and dip the rim of each glass into it, turning to coat. If you want to keep this spicy edge looking neat, a paper napkin can be used to straighten up any messy bits. Make a small slit in the side of each radish, without cutting all the way though.

———

To serve, fill each glass with ice and add 3½ tablespoons of the vodka. Add enough of the tomato mixture to half-fill the glass, then stir; fill it to the top and stir again. Add a pinch of salt and pepper, a sprinkle of nigella seeds, and balance a radish on the rim of the glass.

POMEGRANATE & SUMAC MARTINI

This recipe is a twist on that 1990s classic, the Cosmopolitan. The pomegranate tea we use is from a company called T2 and is available online, but you can use any loose-leaf pomegranate tea for the same effect.

While the pomegranate tea is still hot, add the sugar, stir to dissolve, and leave to cool overnight. At the same time, add 2 tablespoons of the sumac to the vodka and leave it overnight to infuse. About 1 hour before serving, strain the vodka and add the rum, pomegranate juice, and tea syrup. Store it in the refrigerator until required.

———

To serve, fill your cocktail glasses with ice and water, leave to chill for 2 minutes, then empty them. Cut 1 lime into wedges and use it to rub around the top of the glasses. Spread out the remaining sumac in a shallow saucer, then dip the rim of each glass into it, turning to coat the whole rim. If you want to keep the sumac edge looking neat, use a paper napkin to straighten up any messy bits.

———

It's best to make no more than 2 cocktails at a time. To do this, fill a cocktail shaker (or any large screwtop jar) with ice. Add 1 cup (250 ml) of the prepared mixture and the juice of 1 lime. Shake well, until the shaker feels cold to the touch. Strain into the glasses, making sure the ice stays in the shaker. Repeat to make the rest of the cocktails.

SERVES 6

½ cup (120 ml) pomegranate tea, brewed according to the manufacturer's instructions

2–3 tablespoons sugar, to taste

⅓ cup (1½ oz/40 g) sumac

⅔ cup (150 ml) good-quality vodka

⅔ cup (150 ml) spiced rum

1¼ cups (300 ml) pomegranate juice

1 lime, plus the freshly squeezed juice of 3 limes

MEDJOOL DATE, ESPRESSO & FENNEL MARTINI

½ tablespoon fennel seeds

4½ oz (125 g) dried dates (about 5)

¾ cup (175 ml) boiling water

⅔ cup (150 ml) good-quality vodka

⅔ cup (150 ml) brandy

1½ cups (350 ml) espresso or strong coffee

candied dates, to garnish (optional)

Espresso martinis have become a staple of good cocktail lists, and we have added our own Oklava touch. At the restaurant we use a Cypriot brandy called Anglias, which is available online, but any good-quality brandy would do. If you don't have an espresso machine, we recommend brewing a strong, full-bodied coffee in a French press and letting it sit for 30 minutes or so, straining it before use. You can add a garnish of candied dates to the rim, if you like, but this requires some advance preparation: coat sliced dried dates in sugar syrup, then leave them to harden and cool.

Toast the fennel seeds gently in a dry pan over high heat for 60–90 seconds, or until lightly colored. Finely chop the dried dates—whiz them in the food processor if possible—and combine them in a bowl with the boiling water and the fennel seeds. Leave overnight to infuse. It should make a thick purée, but you might need to water it down slightly to give a pourable consistency.

———

To serve, for each person fill a cocktail shaker or a large screwtop jar with ice and add 1½ tablespoons vodka, 1½ tablespoons brandy, ¼ cup (60 ml) espresso, and 2½ tablespoons date purée. Shake hard for a few minutes to create the signature foamy top, then strain into a cocktail glass, making sure no ice falls into the drink.

CYPRIOT 75

This is our take on the classic French 75 champagne cocktail. We use Cypriot brandy, but any good-quality brandy would do; the apple tea still gives it a Turkish feel. You could use our recipe for it (see page 169) or use a store-bought sweet apple tea. We serve this cocktail in wine glasses, but you could use champagne flutes, rocks glasses, or wine glasses—whatever you prefer.

When the apple tea is cool, mix it with the brandy and refrigerate until required.

———

To serve, pour ⅓ cup (80 ml) of the brandy mixture into each glass and top up with ½ cup (120 ml) sparkling wine. Hang the thyme sprig over the rim or stick it in like a straw.

SERVES 6

1¼ cups (300 ml) apple tea, brewed according to the packet instructions

⅔ cup (150 ml) brandy

3 cups (700 ml) sparkling wine (we recommend Turkish, of course)

6 sprigs of thyme

RAKI

Rakı (pronounced "rack-ur") is considered by many to be the national drink of Turkey, and is famous world over. Produced by distilling grape pomace and flavored with aniseed, rakı is similar to other famous drinks from neighboring countries, and has a somewhat fearsome reputation outside Turkey thanks to its nickname, "lion's milk." Although we might more commonly think of spirits as a digestif, rakı is a popular aperitif and is also often drunk throughout a meal. We serve it at the restaurant as an aperitif, with cold water and ice cubes on the side; when water is added, the liquid will turn cloudy, an effect that led to its nickname.

Rakı is often grouped with certain spirits that many of us "enjoyed" ill-advisedly as youths, such as sambuca. As a result, we find that some guests are reluctant to try it, but the addition of water brings out a softer, sweeter side to the spirit, and it is sure to be a talking point at any meal. Traditionally, rakı is drunk alongside mezze or fish and is said to have been a favorite of the founder and first president of the Republic of Turkey, Mustafa Kemal Atatürk. We serve Yeni rakı, which is one of the most famous brands and widely available all over the world. It is a new style of rakı with a distinctive bitter taste, and we recommend putting a bottle of it on the dinner table, along with a jug of water and a small ice bucket, to accompany your appetizers and tempt your guests into trying something new.

MEDJOOL DATE BUTTER

The secret is finally revealed! No one has ever been able to work out what the magic flavor in our butter is, and fair enough: since my food is all about Turkish flavors, you'd never expect it to be black rice vinegar. I first made this when some friends of mine were coming over for a final meal before heading back to New Zealand. They are two big lovers of bread and butter, so I wanted to produce the most delicious butter I could make. Looking around for inspiration, I spotted some Medjool dates sitting in a black vinegar syrup, so I decided to whiz some into a block of butter. A year or so later, after serving it at one of my first pop-ups, I realized it was a huge hit: everyone kept asking for more and I ended up running out, even though I'd made twice as much as I thought I needed.

Put the dates with the sugar and vinegar in a small pan over medium heat and cook until slightly jam like; crush the dates a little as you go. Allow the date mixture to cool completely, then combine it with the soft butter. Transfer it to a container or mold and leave to set in the refrigerator. Serve with a little flaky sea salt sprinkled on top.

MAKES ABOUT
1 LB 9 OZ (700 G)

7 oz (200 g) Medjool dates, pitted (about 8)

1 heaped tablespoon sugar

2½ tablespoons black rice vinegar (available in Asian supermarkets)

4½ sticks (1 lb 2 oz/500 g) unsalted butter, softened

flaky sea salt

CHILI BUTTER

Olive oil is widely used in Turkish cooking, but in certain parts of Turkey, butter is the leading fat in the kitchen.

Melt the butter in a pan over medium heat and keep it there until it turns nut brown. Strain it through a fine sieve into a large heatproof container and add the pepper flakes immediately (it will puff up, hence the need for a large container). Stir in the olive oil, then set aside to cool completely before storing in the refrigerator.

MAKES ABOUT
9 OZ (250 G)

2¼ sticks (9 oz/250 g) unsalted butter

2 tablespoons Aleppo pepper flakes (pul biber)

3½ tablespoons extra-virgin olive oil

LIME MAYONNAISE

We serve lime mayonnaise alongside our chili-garlic chicken; the subtle zing is a real winner. If you're short on time, you could just buy a good-quality Indian lime pickle instead of making your own.

First make the lime pickle: you will need a pressure cooker. Mix the limes with the salt in a non-reactive container and put in the refrigerator for 5 days, stirring once a day. Rinse the limes with cold water and set aside.

Put the sugar in the pressure cooker and heat, uncovered, until it forms a dark brown caramel. Remove the pan from the heat and add the mustard and coriander seeds. As they start to pop, carefully add the limes; the mixture will spit. Cook over medium heat for about 5 minutes, or until you see the juice coming out of the limes.

Put the lid on and gently bring the pan up to pressure. When you hear it hissing, reduce the heat to its lowest setting and cook for 15 minutes. Remove the pan from the heat and allow the pressure to drop completely before opening the lid. Add the vinegar and continue to cook, uncovered, until it is the consistency of chutney. Allow it to cool, then roughly whiz in a food processor before transferring it to a sterilized jar. Store in the refrigerator.

To make the mayonnaise, whisk the egg yolks with the mustard, vinegar, and lime juice until well incorporated. (You can do this with a hand-held electric mixer or by hand with a balloon whisk.) While continuing to whisk, slowly drizzle in the oil. Finish by adding the lime pickle and season with salt.

**MAKES ABOUT
2 CUPS (450 ML)**

2 large egg yolks

½ teaspoon Dijon mustard

1½ tablespoons white wine vinegar

freshly squeezed juice of ½ lime

1¼ cups (300 ml) sunflower oil

fine salt

FOR THE LIME PICKLE

10 limes, cut into quarters

1½ tablespoons fine salt

¾ cup (5½ oz/150 g) sugar

2 tablespoons black mustard seeds

¼ cup (¾ oz/20 g) coriander seeds, lightly crushed

scant ½ cup (100 ml) red wine vinegar

URFA CHILI MAYONNAISE

This mayonnaise totally surprised me when we first made it, because the Urfa chili gives it an almost coffee-like flavor in the background. Serve with any meats or poultry, or even to dress a potato salad.

Put the egg yolks, vinegar, garlic, and Urfa pepper in a food processor and blend together well. With the motor still running, slowly drizzle in the oil until a mayonnaise is formed. Season with salt.

**MAKES 2 LB 4 OZ
(1 KG)**

generous ½ cup (5½ oz/150 g) egg yolks (about 9)

⅓ cup (80 ml) moscatel vinegar

½–1 garlic clove

¼ cup (1 oz/30 g) Urfa red pepper flakes (isot biber)

3⅓ cups (800 ml) sunflower oil

fine salt

BLACK OLIVE & PEPPER TAPENADE

SERVES 4–6

6 tablespoons (90 ml) extra-virgin olive oil

2 garlic cloves, thinly sliced

1 teaspoon thyme, leaves only

2 tablespoons sherry vinegar or red wine vinegar

¼ cup (2¼ oz/60 g) black olive paste

2 heaped tablespoons Turkish hot pepper paste (açi biber salçasi)

fine salt

Black olive paste is available in Turkish supermarkets. It's great as part of a breakfast spread—I love it on hot toast.

Heat the oil and garlic gently in a small saucepan. When the garlic starts to turn a little brown around the edges, take the pan off the heat and add the thyme and vinegar. Combine with the two pastes, then season with salt. This will keep in the refrigerator for up to 3 weeks.

TOMATO RELISH

MAKES 10½ OZ

(300 G)

1 banana shallot, finely diced

small bunch of chives, thinly sliced

2 sprigs of tarragon, leaves only, finely chopped

1 teaspoon Urfa red pepper flakes (isot biber)

1 cup (7 oz/200 g) ketchup

1 teaspoon sugar

2 tablespoons moscatel vinegar

⅓ cup (80 ml) sunflower oil

fine salt

This is essentially glorified ketchup, and it goes really well with anything meaty or fishy.

Whisk together all the ingredients and season with salt. The relish will keep for up to 3 weeks in a clean, well-sealed jar.

MUHAMMARA

My recipe is slightly different from most in that I don't use roasted peppers, but add plenty of pepper paste instead. I love Turkish pepper paste—it's so versatile. Serve *muhammara* as a dip, on toast, or any way you like.

Put all the ingredients except the olive oil and salt in a food processor and blend to a coarse purée. With the motor still running, slowly drizzle in the olive oil. Season with salt.

———

The muhammara will keep up for up to a month in a clean, well-sealed jar.

MAKES 2 LB 4 OZ
(1 KG)

2½ cups (9 oz/250 g) walnuts, toasted

¾ cup (1¾ oz/50 g) fresh breadcrumbs

¼ cup (2¾ oz/75 g) Turkish sweet pepper paste (tatli biber salçasi)

1½ garlic cloves

1 tablespoon Aleppo pepper flakes (pul biber)

1 teaspoon ground cumin

freshly squeezed juice of 1 lemon

2 tablespoons pomegranate molasses

1 heaped tablespoon sugar

1½ cups (375 ml) olive oil

fine salt

WHIPPED FETA

This is great as part of a mezze platter or, as we serve it, on some crostini topped with a slice of candied pumpkin and sprinkled with Aleppo pepper flakes (*pul biber*) and shredded mint. Finish the crostini with flaky sea salt and a drizzle of olive oil.

Blend the cheese and cream to a smooth consistency in a food processor. Store in an airtight container in the refrigerator for up to 1 week.

MAKES 1 LB 2 OZ
(500 G)

14 oz (400 g) Turkish white cheese or feta, crumbled

scant 1 cup (200 ml) heavy cream

Opposite: Muhammara (top left) served as a dip with flatbread, and Whipped Feta, topped with candied pumpkin, Aleppo pepper flakes (pul biber), and shredded mint.

BAHARAT

MAKES ABOUT 1 CUP
(3 ¼ OZ/90 G)

⅓ cup (1 oz/30 g) allspice
berries

⅓ cup (1 oz/30 g) cloves

2½ tablespoons (½ oz/15 g)
mahlep (dried cherry
seeds, available at Turkish
supermarkets)

1 x ¼ oz (10 g) piece nutmeg
(1 large nut)

1 x ⅛ oz (5 g) piece of mastic
(a ¼ in/3 cm piece)

Baharat is often sold as "mixed spice" in Turkish supermarkets. This recipe is based on my grandma's, and is what she uses in her bread. I started off using it just in bread too, although I have now found other great ways to use it. It goes particularly well with fish.

This recipe features some unusual ingredients. Mahlep are dried cherry seeds, which have a bitter flavor but are great when used in the right proportion. Mastic (also called Arabic gum) is the resin from the mastic tree. It has a very unusual taste—almost like pine—and works very well in bread, since it gives it great elasticity. It's quite expensive, but you don't need a lot. You can leave out these ingredients if you can't find them.

———

Blend together all the spices in a spice grinder until fine. Alternatively, if you don't have a spice grinder, buy what you can find in ground form, and grind what you can't using a mortar and pestle. Stored in an airtight container, this will keep for up to 4 weeks.

SUMAC DRESSING

This is the dressing we use for our chili-roasted cauliflower, but it would also be great as a salad dressing.

Put all the ingredients in a blender and process until smooth. Stored in the refrigerator, this dressing will keep for up to 3 weeks.

MAKES 1½ CUPS
(350 ML)

3 garlic cloves, finely grated

freshly squeezed juice of
   2 lemons

1¼ cups (300 ml) extra-virgin
   olive oil

1 tablespoon sumac

fine salt

CAPER DRESSING

This dressing has a great zing to it. Spoon it over roast lamb, chicken, or even a piece of fish. My favorite pairing is with the Grilled Quails (see page 76).

Mix all the ingredients together and it's ready to go. Stored in the refrigerator, this dressing will keep for 1 week.

MAKES ABOUT 1 CUP
(250 ML)

¼ cup (1½ oz/40 g) Lilliput
   capers, rinsed and roughly
   chopped

3 tablespoons sugar

6 tablespoons moscatel
   vinegar

1 banana shallot, finely diced

small bunch of mint, leaves
   only, chopped

small bunch of cilantro,
   leaves and stalks, chopped

3 tablespoons extra-virgin
   olive oil

POMEGRANATE DRESSING

MAKES 2¾ cups
(650 ML)

½ cup (120 ml) pomegranate molasses

1 cup (250 ml) turnip juice (salgam)

1 cup (250 ml) extra-virgin olive oil

2½ tablespoons red wine vinegar

fine salt

We use this dressing at the restaurant for all the salads that accompany the pides and lahmacun. Our salads are a thing of beauty, if you ask me: we combine a selection of bitter and sweet leaves, herbs, onions, tomatoes, radishes, marinated olives, pickled red cabbage, and anything else that's wonderful and in season. The dressing brings out all those flavors to give a zingy hit and cut through the richness of the pides. However, I would highly recommend coating any salad with this dressing, with or without pides.

Put all the ingredients in a blender and process until smooth. Taste to check the seasoning. Stored in the refrigerator, this dressing will keep for up to 4 weeks.

SHERRY VINEGAR CARAMEL

MAKES 1¼ CUPS
(300 ML)

3 cups (750 ml) sherry vinegar

1 cup (7 oz/200 g) sugar

1⅔ cups (400 ml) water

I love mixing acidic and sweet flavors. This caramel is a perfect balance of the two, and is great drizzled over many savory dishes, to give them a boost of flavor. Try it with grilled fish, or a ragout of chickpeas or beans.

Put the vinegar and sugar in a pan with the water and bring to a boil. Simmer to reduce it to a light syrup.

When you think it is ready, drizzle a little onto a plate and put it in the refrigerator for 5 minutes to test it. If the syrup just holds its shape on the plate without running too much, it is ready.

MARINATED OLIVES

My mom is obsessed with green olives from Cyprus. She would often bring back as many as she could carry from her summer visits, then prepare them in batches using this recipe. I love dipping bread into all the juices.

Mix all the ingredients together in a large, sterilized screwtop jar or airtight container and leave to macerate for at least 1 day before eating. The olives will keep for up to 3 weeks.

MAKES 2 LB 4 OZ
(1 KG)

1 lb 2 oz (500 g) black olives (preferably Turkish), rinsed

1 lb 2 oz (500 g) green olives (preferably Turkish), rinsed

¼ cup (¾ oz/20 g) dried oregano, preferably wild

4 garlic cloves, lightly crushed

generous 2 cups (500 g) extra-virgin olive oil

zest (in strips) and freshly squeezed juice from 2 lemons

2 tablespoons coriander seeds, toasted and lightly crushed

PICKLED RED CABBAGE

We use this in the salad that is served with all our *pides*. I like to use this pickle recipe for any vegetables, not just red cabbage: simply pour the pickling liquid over your chosen veggies while still hot and leave for a minimum of 3 days.

Put the water in a pan along with 3 cups (750 ml) of the vinegar, the sugar, spices, and salt and bring to a boil. Simmer for 5 minutes. Remove from the heat and add the remaining vinegar. Strain over the red cabbage and cover with a lid. Once cool, transfer it to a sterilized jar and store in the refrigerator for 3 days before eating. The pickled cabbage will keep for up to 8 weeks.

MAKES 4 LB 8 OZ
(2 KG)

8½ cups (2 liters) water

4¼ cups (1 liter) cider vinegar

2¼ cups (1 lb 2 oz/500 g) sugar

6 cloves

2 star anise

1 tablespoon fine salt

1 red cabbage, thinly sliced (preferably using a mandoline)

FRIED DRIED CHILI YOGURT

**MAKES A GENEROUS
2 CUPS (500 G)**

1 tablespoon sunflower oil

2 tablespoons extra-virgin
olive oil

2 hot dried red chili peppers

generous 2 cups (500 g)
Turkish or Greek yogurt

freshly squeezed juice of
½ lemon

fine salt

This is inspired by the delicious (and very hot) fried dried chilies that are served alongside fried liver in the city of Edirne.

Heat the sunflower oil in a small frying pan over high heat. Add the chilies and cook until they change color, turn a little darker, and become crisp. Allow to cool, then roughly chop them.

Once cooled, place in a bowl, whisk in the remaining ingredients, and season with salt.

ÇEMEN

**MAKES ABOUT
2 CUPS (2 LB 4 OZ/
1 KG)**

¼ cup (1 oz/25 g) ground
fenugreek

4 garlic cloves, peeled

3 tablespoons sugar

⅔ cup (2¾ oz/75 g) paprika

3½ tablespoons (1 oz/25 g) hot
smoked paprika

½ cup (2 oz/50 g) sweet
smoked paprika

1½ tablespoons ground cumin

3½ tablespoons extra-virgin
olive oil

1¼ cups (300 ml) water

Çemen is Turkish for fenugreek but the word is also used to refer to this spice paste. It is most commonly eaten as part of *Kayseri pastirma*, a type of cured beef that is salted, pressed, and air-dried before being smeared all over with *çemen* and left to cure. I adore it and struggle to stop eating it once I have started. I have figured out that the thing I love most about *pastirma* is the flavor of the *çemen*, so I have made my own version and now use it in all sorts of recipes.

Put the fenugreek in bowl, pour in enough water to cover by 1 in (2.5 cm), and stir together. Leave to soak for 10 minutes, then drain off the excess water. Put the fenugreek and all the remaining ingredients in a food processor—it's best to add the garlic first, then put everything else on top—and blend to a fine purée. The paste will keep for up to 3 months, stored in an airtight container in the refrigerator.

ORANGE CREAM

We use this orange cream at the restaurant as an accompaniment to our Chocolate Delice (see page 212). When they're in season, we like to use bergamot oranges to make it.

Put the orange zest, milk, and 3½ tablespoons of the cream in a pan and bring to a boil. Meanwhile, whisk the eggs, egg yolk, sugar, and cornstarch until pale and fluffy. Still whisking, pour the hot milk mixture into the egg mixture. Return it to the pan and cook, whisking continuously, over medium heat for 4-5 minutes, or until thickened and the cornstarch has cooked out. Take the pan off the heat and add the butter in 3 batches, ensuring that each batch melts in before adding the next.

———

Soak the gelatin in cold water, then add it to the warm custard mixture, whisking until it dissolves. Allow it to cool completely. Whip the remaining cream to soft peaks. Finally, stir the orange juice into the custard mixture and fold in the whipped cream.

MAKES 3 ½ CUPS
(1 LB 12 OZ/800 G)

grated zest and juice of 2 oranges (bergamot or blood oranges can be used, if available)

1¾ cups (400 ml) milk

¾ cup (175 ml) heavy cream

2 large eggs, plus 1 large egg yolk

⅓ cup (2¾ oz/75 g) sugar

½ cup (2¼ oz/60 g) cornstarch

7 tablespoons (3½ oz/100 g) unsalted butter, diced

¾ teaspoon unflavored gelatin powder

ORANGE BLOSSOM SYRUP

This syrup is great on French toast, pancakes, or any lovely Turkish dessert that calls for syrup.

Put all the ingredients, except the orange blossom water, in a pan and bring to a boil. Simmer until it reaches a syrupy consistency. Remove from the heat and add the orange blossom water. Leave the spices in to keep infusing until you use the syrup. Stored in the refrigerator, this syrup will keep for up to 3 months.

MAKES 1 CUP
(250 ML)

1¼ cups (9 oz/250 g) sugar

2 teaspoons vanilla extract

1 teaspoon cloves

3 star anise

generous ½ cup (140 ml) water

1-2 tablespoons orange blossom water

PRESERVED LEMONS

MAKES 3 LB 5 OZ (1.5 KG)

10 lemons, quartered
2½ tablespoons fine salt
3 tablespoons flaky sea salt
2 bay leaves
4 sprigs of thyme

Preserved lemons are readily available these days, but it's so easy to make your own. I highly recommend trying this recipe and stashing them away to jazz up your meals.

Mix all the ingredients together, slightly squishing the lemons as you go. Put them in a large sterilized jar or lidded container, seal tightly, and put them in the refrigerator. Leave to macerate for 4 weeks, turning the container upside down every day. The lemons will keep for up to 3 months.

SWEET
THINGS

SEMOLINA CUSTARD & FILO BÖREK

You can serve these pastries as they are (they're best slightly warm), or with some ice cream and a few pistachios for extra indulgence. The recipe for *sütlü börek* I've given here is a slight variation of one of my mom's, to which I've added vanilla and orange blossom because I think it tastes nicer. Mom isn't convinced, and thinks that the traditional way is the best, so I invite you to try it both ways and judge for yourself.

First make the syrup: put the water in a pan with the sugar and bring to a boil. Simmer until it takes on a syrupy consistency and is slightly sticky. Add the lemon juice and the orange blossom water, if using. Leave to cool completely.

To make the filling, mix the semolina and cornstarch with just under 1 cup (about 200 ml) of the milk to make a smooth paste. Put the remaining milk in a pan with the sugar and heat to just below boiling point. Whisk the semolina mixture into the hot milk and reduce the heat to medium. Add the vanilla and keep whisking until you have a very thick custard. Immediately pour it into a shallow tray measuring about 16 x 12 in (40 x 30 cm). Allow the mixture to cool, then cut it, still in the tray, into 18-20 equal rectangular pieces.

Preheat the oven to 425°F (220°C) and line 2 large baking sheets with parchment paper. Take 1 sheet of filo pastry and fold it in half to form a small rectangle. Place it in front of you short end up. Brush it all over with butter. Now place a rectangle of the custard in the middle of the edge closest to you and fold it over once, working away from you, to enclose it in the pastry. Fold in each side of the pastry on the left and right. Brush the sides with butter and continue folding over until you reach the end of the pastry, sealing it with a little butter. It is important to fold quite tightly around the custard and ensure there are no cracks for it to escape. If any cracks do form, wrap the whole thing in another sheet of filo.

Place the börek on a prepared baking sheet and repeat the folding process with the rest of the filo and custard. Leave a ¾ in (2 cm) gap between each pastry. Brush the tops with butter and bake until golden brown all over, about 20 minutes. When you take them out of the oven, submerge them one at a time in the cold syrup and transfer to a serving dish. Sprinkle with the pistachios, if using. Allow to cool before serving.

MAKES 18–20

20 sheets of filo pastry
1¾ sticks (7 oz/200 g) unsalted butter, melted
¾ cup (3½ oz/100 g) shelled pistachios, toasted and crushed (optional)

FOR THE FILLING

1½ cups (9 oz/250 g) semolina
heaped ¼ cup (3½ oz/100 g) cornstarch
5 cups (1.2 liters) milk
3 heaped tablespoons sugar
1 teaspoon vanilla extract

FOR THE SYRUP

generous 2 cups (500 ml) water
2½ cups (1 lb 2 oz/500 g) sugar
freshly squeezed juice of ½ lemon
2 teaspoons orange blossom water (optional)

SPICED RICE PUDDING BRÛLÉE WITH PISTACHIOS, CARAMELIZED PINEAPPLE, RUM JELLO, LYCHEES & CANDIED LIME ZEST

SERVES 8–10

brown sugar, for sprinkling

¾ cup (3½ oz/100 g) shelled pistachios, toasted and crushed

FOR THE RICE PUDDING

6 cups (1.4 liters) milk

½ cup (3½ oz/100 g) sugar

2 cinnamon sticks (6 in/15 cm total)

1 tablespoon star anise

1 tablespoon cloves

1 teaspoon vanilla extract

generous ¾ cup (5½ oz/150 g) arborio rice

scant 1 cup (200 ml) heavy cream

FOR THE RUM JELLO

¾ teaspoon unflavored gelatin powder

½ cup (120 ml) water

2 tablespoons brown sugar

2 tablespoons rum

FOR THE LYCHEES

grated zest and freshly squeezed juice of 1 lime

1½ tablespoons grated ginger

6 oz (175 g) drained canned lychees (about 20), halved

FOR THE CANDIED LIME ZEST

2 limes

6 tablespoons (2¾ oz/75 g) sugar

3½ tablespoons water

FOR THE CARAMELIZED PINEAPPLE

¼ cup (1¾ oz/50 g) sugar

½ fresh pineapple, peeled, cored, and diced into ¾ in (2 cm) pieces

1 tablespoon (½ oz/15 g) unsalted butter

2 tablespoons tamarind paste

This dish is inspired by *sütlaç*, a traditional creamy spiced rice pudding, and it has converted many a rice-pudding doubter. There are a lot of garnishes, but the rice pudding is tasty just on its own, so make as few or as many of the extras as you like. If you would like to make your own tamarind paste, buy fresh tamarind (with seeds), simmer them in water until soft, then pass through a sieve.

First make the rice pudding: put the milk, sugar, spices, and vanilla in a pan and bring gently to a simmer. Remove from the heat and cover the pan with plastic wrap. Leave to infuse for 30 minutes. Strain the milk into a new pan and add the rice. Cook, stirring occasionally, over low heat for about 30 minutes, or until the rice is soft. Leave the rice to cool (it will still look quite watery but will firm up), then chill completely.

Whip the cream to soft peaks and fold it through the cooled rice pudding. Divide between 8–10 ramekins or bowls and return to the refrigerator until needed.

To make the rum jello, put the gelatin powder into ¼ cup (60 ml) cold water and set aside to soak. Heat the sugar and ¼ cup (60 ml) water in a pan, bring to a boil, and simmer for 2 minutes. Remove the pan from the heat and add the rum and soaking gelatin, stirring to dissolve. Remove from the heat, leave to cool, then store in the refrigerator.

To make the lychees, mix the ingredients in a bowl, then set aside.

To make the candied lime zest, peel the limes, scrape off the pith, and slice the zest into very fine strips. Put the sugar and water in a pan and bring to a boil. Add the strips of lime zest, reduce the heat to a very gentle simmer, and cook until a thick syrup forms. Drain off the syrup and leave the lime zest to cool on a rack or a tray lined with parchment paper.

To make the caramelized pineapple, put the sugar in a large heavy-based pan or non-stick frying pan, and add a dash of water to make a paste. Cook over medium heat without stirring until a dark caramel forms, then immediately and carefully add the pineapple. The caramel will clump together a little, so keep cooking until it all turns liquid again. Add the butter and keep cooking until most of the liquid has evaporated. Add the tamarind paste, transfer to a container, and leave to cool.

To assemble, sprinkle a thin layer of brown sugar evenly over each rice pudding. Use a blowtorch or very hot broiler to caramelize the sugar golden-brown. Allow the caramelized sugar to cool, then sprinkle on the pistachios, followed by some pineapple and lychees. Now place 4–5 small spoonfuls of rum jello on each pudding. Finish with a few strands of candied lime zest.

TRILECE CAKE

I first tried *trilece* cake in Istanbul when it was brought to us as a complimentary dessert by a waiter who was very much taken with Laura. I thought it was delicious, and the waiter told me it was a traditional Balkan dessert. I later found out that this cake is in fashion in Istanbul, with restaurants across the city trying to out-do each other with their versions. The cake is almost cookie-like once baked, so quite a dry texture, but this allows it to soak up all the flavor from the milk to produce a delicious moist sponge. I like to serve this cake with some Medjool dates, which I coat in a little of the caramel topping and finish with a dollop of *kaymak* (Turkish clotted cream).

Preheat the oven to 400°F (200°C) and grease a 12 x 10 x 2 in (30 x 25 x 5 cm) baking pan, or 12 individual baking rings, 3 in (8 cm) diameter.

———

Whisk the egg whites to soft peaks in a large bowl. Add the sugar in 3 batches, whisking constantly to ensure that each batch is fully incorporated before adding the next. Whisk in the egg yolks one at a time, followed by the vanilla extract.

———

Fold in the flour and baking powder until fully incorporated. I use a whisk to do this, but folding rather than whisking. Carefully pour the batter into the prepared pan or rings and bake until golden brown and springy. Individual cakes will take about 12 minutes and a whole pan will take about 30 minutes.

———

While the cake bakes, mix together the ingredients for the soaking liquid. When the cake comes out of the oven, pour the cold mixture over the hot cake and allow it to cool completely and absorb the liquid for about 4 hours. Once cool, cut the cake into 12 equal pieces.

———

To make the caramel, put the glucose and sugar in a heavy-based pan or non-stick frying pan and cook over medium heat until it becomes a dark caramel. Taking great care, since it will spit, slowly pour in the water. The caramel will seize up, but keep cooking until it all turns to liquid again. Continue heating the caramel until it becomes a fairly thick syrup. To test it, pour a little onto a saucer and place in the fridge for 5 minutes—the caramel should still be a little runny once cool. If it isn't, it has gone too far, so add a little more water and bring it back up to a boil. Allow the caramel to cool completely before pouring it over the cake, keeping back a little to garnish each serving. To serve, put a piece of cake on each plate and drizzle a little extra caramel around it. Add some Medjool dates dipped in caramel, then top with a dollop of cream.

SERVES 12

sunflower oil, for greasing

4 large eggs, separated

1 cup (7 oz/200 g) superfine sugar

2 teaspoons vanilla extract

2¼ cups (9¾ oz/270 g) all-purpose flour, sifted

1½ teaspoons baking powder, sifted

FOR THE SOAKING LIQUID

generous 2 cups (500 ml) cow, goat, or sheep milk

1 cup (250 ml) heavy cream

1 cup (250 ml) condensed milk

FOR THE CARAMEL

scant 1 cup (10½ oz/300 g) liquid glucose

¾ cup (5½ oz/150 g) sugar

1 cup (250 ml) water

TO SERVE

Medjool dates

kaymak (Turkish clotted cream)

DARK CHOCOLATE & PRALINE KATMER WITH PISTACHIOS

SERVES 1–2

1 sheet of filo pastry, about
14½ x 12 in (37 x 30 cm)

2 tablespoons (1 oz/25 g)
unsalted butter, melted

5 teaspoons praline paste or
Nutella

½ oz (15 g) good-quality
dark chocolate (70% cocoa
solids), roughly chopped

⅓ cup (1½ oz/40 g) shelled
pistachios, toasted and
chopped

Praline is one of my guilty pleasures, particularly in the form of a certain shell-shaped chocolate. *Katmer* is a specialty dish from Gaziantep in south-eastern Anatolia, traditionally filled with *kaymak*, which is a Turkish clotted cream, and pistachios, and often served as a breakfast dish alongside a cup of Turkish tea. Traditionally the pastry is handmade by expert bakers, who stretch it out thinner than a bedsheet before folding it into a multi-layered square with the filling in the center. Using ready-made filo pastry makes this recipe much more feasible for the non-expert, and the chocolate and praline filling makes it a perfect indulgent weekend brunch dish. This recipe makes just one *katmer*, but it is easily scaled up to make as many as you desire.

Brush the filo sheet with a little of the melted butter. Place the praline in 5 dots in a square formation in the center of the sheet. Sprinkle with the chocolate and half of the pistachios.

———

Starting at the top left, fold the corner into the center, then fold the bottom right corner in to meet it. Fold in the two remaining corners, overlapping them in the middle to end up with a square.

———

Place a large frying pan over medium-high heat and add the remaining melted butter. Place the katmer in the pan, seam-side down. Cook for 1–2 minutes on each side, or until golden and crisp. Serve with the rest of the pistachios sprinkled over the top.

CHOCOLATE, PRUNE & CARDAMOM DELICE

This rich layered dessert, gently spiced with cardamom, will appeal to chocoholics and fans of fruity desserts alike.

First make the poached prunes: put the water in a pan with the sugar, mastic, vanilla, orange zest, wine, and tea leaves and bring to a boil. Simmer until it reaches a light syrup consistency. Strain into a container, add the prunes, and leave to steep for at least 1 hour. Strain the liquid into a pan and simmer to reduce to a thick syrup. Process half the prunes to a coarse purée using a stick blender, and set aside. Put the rest of the prunes into a container, pour in the thick syrup, and set aside.

———

Place a stainless steel cake mold, about 12 x 8 in (30 x 20 cm), on a baking pan lined with parchment paper.

———

To make the praline, break the milk chocolate and 2¾ oz (75 g) of the dark chocolate into pieces and put it in a heatproof bowl with the praline. Set it over a pan of barely simmering water. Once the chocolate has melted, remove from the heat and stir in the feuilletine or corn flakes. Pour half the mixture into your mold, spread it out in an even layer, then refrigerate to set. Melt the remaining mixture with the remaining dark chocolate, then spread it in a thin layer on a baking pan lined with parchment paper. Cool in the refrigerator.

———

To make the delice, put the milk, cream, and cardamom in a pan and bring to a

boil. Remove from the heat, cover with plastic, and leave to infuse for 1 hour.

———

Once the praline mixture in the mold has set, spread the prune purée over it and return it to the refrigerator.

———

Break the delice chocolate into pieces and melt as before. Strain the cardamom-infused milk mixture and bring it back to a boil. Whisk the egg yolks in a bowl until pale, then slowly pour the hot milk mixture over them, whisking continuously. Return to the pan and set over low heat, whisking until it has thickened to a custard consistency. Pour it over the melted chocolate, whisking continuously. Pour the mixture into the mold on top of the prune purée. Return it to the refrigerator to set.

———

Now make the chocolate glaze: soak the gelatin in the cold water until softened. Meanwhile, put the cream, sugar, and cocoa in a pan and whisk together. Bring to a boil, whisking all the time, until slightly sticky. Remove the pan from the heat, add the gelatin and water, and whisk until dissolved. Strain into a bowl and allow to cool to room temperature.

———

Evenly spread the glaze over the delice. Return to the refrigerator to set. Using a blowtorch or over the burner, heat the mold just enough to release it and lift it off. Using a hot knife, cut the delice into 16–24 pieces. Serve the delice with the whole prunes, shards of praline, a dollop of orange cream, and a drizzle of leftover glaze, if you have some.

SERVES 16–24

generous ½ cup (140 ml) milk

1⅓ cups (325 ml) heavy cream

2 teaspoons cardamom pods, toasted and crushed

12 oz (340 g) good-quality dark chocolate

½ cup (4¼ oz/120 g) egg yolks (about 7)

1 quantity Orange Cream (see page 200), to serve

FOR THE POACHED PRUNES

¾ cup (175 ml) water

6 tablespoons (2¾ oz/75 g) sugar

a lentil-size piece (1 g) mastic (Arabic gum)

2½ teaspoons vanilla extract

grated zest of 1 orange, bergamot variety if possible

½ cup (120 ml) white wine

2 teaspoons Earl Grey tea leaves

1¾ cups (9 oz/250 g) prunes

FOR THE PRALINE

2¾ oz (75 g) good-quality milk chocolate

4½ oz (125 g) good-quality dark chocolate

4 teaspoons praline paste or Nutella

3½ cups (3½ oz/100 g) feuilletine or cornflakes, crushed

FOR THE CHOCOLATE GLAZE

1 x ¼ oz (7 g) envelope unflavored gelatin powder

scant ½ cup (100 ml) cold water

generous ½ cup (140 ml) heavy cream

1 cup (7 oz/200 g) sugar

1 cup (3¼ oz/90 g) unsweetened cocoa powder

RICOTTA & VANILLA KADAYIF WITH BERGAMOT CREAM & STRAWBERRIES

SERVES 8

14 oz (400 g) kadayif pastry (available in Turkish supermarkets)

1½ sticks (6 oz/170 g) unsalted butter, melted

⅔ cup (5¾ oz/160 g) ricotta

1 teaspoon vanilla extract

1 quantity Orange Blossom Syrup (see page 200)

16 strawberries, trimmed and halved

FOR THE BERGAMOT CREAM

⅔ cup (5¾ oz/160 g) mascarpone

grated zest of ½ orange

½ teaspoon vanilla extract

1 heaped tablespoon candied bergamot (available online), finely chopped, or bergamot jam

Kadayif **is best described as shredded filo pastry, and it is used in many ways to create syrup-based desserts. You're aiming for a pastry that is soaked in syrup but retains some crunch; it shouldn't be soggy. The bergamot cream adds sharpness and the strawberries a freshness to balance out the indulgence of the syrupy ricotta pastry.**

Preheat the oven to 425°F (220°C).

———

Put the pastry into a bowl, pour in the melted butter, and mix very well. Divide the pastry into 8 equal piles, arranging each pile into a long rectangle.

———

Mix the ricotta with the vanilla, divide into 8 equal portions, and place one at the end of each pastry rectangle. Roll up tightly to form 8 cylinders. Place on a baking tray, seam-side down. Bake for 18–20 minutes, or until golden brown and crisp.

———

Meanwhile, combine all the ingredients for the bergamot cream.

———

Remove the pastries from the oven and pour the cold orange blossom syrup all over them, reserving a little syrup to serve. Allow to cool slightly before serving with a spoonful of bergamot cream, a pile of strawberries, and an extra drizzle of orange blossom syrup.

SEMOLINA CAKE

Simit tatlisi is a classic cake in our household. Mom makes it at the end of the Bayram dinners that mark Turkish festivals and national holidays. At Bayram, all the family comes together for a big Turkish roast dinner with all the trimmings. This recipe is slightly lighter and not quite as sweet as a traditional version, which is just as well at the end of a big meal.

First make the syrup. Bring the water and sugar to a boil in a pan. Reduce the heat and simmer until it reaches a syrupy consistency, then add the lemon juice and rose or orange blossom water, if using. Set aside to cool.

Preheat the oven to 425°F (220°C) and lightly oil a baking dish measuring about 10 x 14 in (26 x 36 cm).

To make the cake, put the eggs, vanilla, sugar, and lemon zest in a bowl and whisk until just combined. Add the measured oil and milk. Mix the semolina and baking powder together in a large bowl. Gradually, whisking all the time, add the wet mixture to the semolina to form a smooth batter. Pour it into the prepared dish and scatter the almonds over the surface. Bake for about 30 minutes, or until golden brown and an inserted skewer comes out clean.

Leave the cake to rest for 2 minutes before pouring on the syrup in 4 batches, allowing each batch to be absorbed before adding the next. Once all the syrup has been absorbed, cut the cake into portions.

SERVES 16–20

¾ cup (175 ml) sunflower oil, plus extra for greasing

4 large eggs

1 teaspoon vanilla extract

1¼ cups (9 oz/250 g) sugar

grated zest of 1 lemon

1 cup (250 ml) milk

3 cups (1 lb 2 oz/500 g) coarse semolina

1 tablespoon baking powder

1½ cups (7 oz/200 g) skinned whole almonds, crushed

FOR THE SYRUP

6 cups (1.5 liters) water

2½ cups (1 lb 2 oz/500 g) sugar

freshly squeezed juice of ¼ lemon

1–2 tablespoons rose water or orange blossom water (optional)

BLOOD ORANGE GANACHE, POACHED PEAR & ROSEMARY FILO SHARDS

SERVES 8

generous 2 cups (500 ml) blood orange juice

9½ oz (270 g) good-quality white chocolate

scant 1 cup (200 ml) heavy cream

½ teaspoon vanilla extract

FOR THE POACHED PEAR

4¼ cups (1 liter) water

1 cup (250 ml) white wine

1⅓ cups (13 oz/375 g) sugar

¾ cup (9 oz/250 g) honey

1 strip of lemon peel

1 sprig of thyme

4 pears (I like to use Bartletts)

freshly squeezed juice of ½ lemon

FOR THE DECORATION

4 sheets of filo pastry

3½ tablespoons (1¾ oz/50 g) unsalted butter

confectioner's sugar, for dusting

1 tablespoon rosemary, finely chopped

2 blood oranges, segmented

This blood orange ganache is a real crowd pleaser. It's rich and works well alongside the juicy poached pear and the filo shards that add texture to the dish. At the beginning of the year, when blood oranges are in season, I always include this on the menu.

Bring the orange juice to a boil in a pan and simmer to reduce it to ⅔ cup (150 ml). Meanwhile, put the white chocolate, cream, and vanilla in a heatproof bowl set over a pan of barely simmering water, making sure the bowl doesn't touch the water. Leave it to melt, then remove from the heat and let it cool slightly. Once the white chocolate mixture and reduced orange juice are about the same temperature, whisk them together. Transfer to a container and place in the refrigerator to set.

To poach the pears, put the water in a pan with the wine, sugar, honey, lemon zest, and thyme and bring to a boil. Reduce the heat and simmer until it reaches a light syrup consistency. Meanwhile, peel the pears, cut them in half, and remove the core with a spoon. Rub them with the lemon juice to prevent discoloration. Once all the pears are prepared, add them carefully to the poaching liquid and cover with a piece of parchment paper sitting directly on top of the liquid.

Reduce the heat to its lowest setting and poach for about 15 minutes, or until the pears are just soft (use a knife to test them). Remove the fruit and simmer the liquid to reduce it to a thicker syrup consistency. Set aside to cool, then pour it over the pears.

Preheat the oven to 425°F (220°C). To make filo shards, take 1 sheet of filo and brush it with melted butter. Dust it with confectioner's sugar, sprinkle over some rosemary, then place another sheet of filo over the top. Repeat the process twice more, brushing and sprinkling between each one, but brush the very top with butter only. Place the filo "sandwich" between 2 sheets of parchment paper, then slide it onto a flat baking tray and put another (preferably identical) baking tray on top. Bake for 6 minutes, then check to see if the filo is golden brown and crisp. You will probably need to cook it for another 5 minutes, but keep checking it. Remove the top baking sheet and set the filo aside to cool.

To serve, put half a poached pear on each plate (if you have a blowtorch, you could lightly glaze the cut side). Put a spoonful of ganache next to the pear, break off a shard of filo, and poke it into the ganache. Decorate each plate with fresh orange segments and serve.

MUHALLEBI WITH STRAWBERRY JELLO

Muhallebi is a milk pudding thickened with cornstarch. It was my dad's favorite dessert, so there was often a bowl of this sitting in the refrigerator when I was growing up. Traditionally, it is served with rosewater syrup or a sprinkling of ground cinnamon. I think the addition of strawberry jello, which is inspired by my chef college mentor Vince Cottam, is very good. Vince coached me through several culinary competitions, and a berry-based soup was sometimes included in our desserts. I've adjusted the recipe here to make the berry soup into a jello.

In a small bowl, mix the cornstarch with a scant 1 cup (200 ml) of the milk. Put the rest of the milk in a pan and bring gently to a boil. Reduce the heat and whisk in the cornstarch mixture, vanilla extract, and the sugar. Continue whisking until it turns into a thick custard, then pour it straight into your serving glasses or dishes, and leave to cool. Once cool, put it in the refrigerator to set.

To make the jello, mix the berries with the confectioner's sugar and vanilla in a heatproof bowl and cover it tightly with plastic wrap. Set the bowl over a pan of simmering water and leave for 30 minutes: the juices will be released from the fruits. Transfer to a sieve set over a jug and leave until all the juices have run out. You can push very gently on the fruits to help the process along, but don't push too hard, or the juice will become cloudy.

The amount of liquid released from your fruit will determine how much gelatin powder you need. For ½ cup (120 ml) liquid you will typically need 1 teaspoon (check the package instructions). Soak the correct amount of gelatin in half of the cold berry juice until softened. Heat the rest of the juice in a pan to just below boiling point, then remove from the heat, and add the gelatin and cold juice to the hot liquid. Whisk to dissolve the gelatin and allow to cool. Once it is completely cold, divide it between the muhallebi dishes and return them to the refrigerator to set. Serve with fresh berries on top.

SERVES 4–6

3 heaped tablespoons cornstarch

2½ cups (580 ml) milk

1 teaspoon vanilla extract

3 heaped tablespoons sugar

1½ cups (7 oz/200 g) mixed berries, washed and sliced, to decorate

FOR THE STRAWBERRY JELLO

1¼ cups (5½ oz/150 g) raspberries

2 cups (10½ oz/300 g) strawberries, trimmed

1¼ cups (5½ oz/150 g) redcurrants (or use more of the other berries)

¼ cup (1 oz/30 g) confectioner's sugar

½ vanilla bean, halved lengthways and seeds scraped out

1–1½ teaspoons unflavored gelatin powder

SYRUP SPONGE CAKE STUFFED WITH RICOTTA & WALNUTS

SERVES 10–12

1 package ekmek kadayif (a kind of dry sponge cake, available at Turkish supermarkets), about 10 in (25 cm) in diameter, sliced in half horizontally

3½ tablespoons rose water or orange blossom water (optional)

2 cups (1 lb 2 oz/500 g) ricotta

3 cups (10½ oz/300 g) walnuts, toasted and crushed

FOR THE SYRUP

6 cups (1.5 liters) water

5 cups (2 lb 4 oz/1 kg) sugar

2 cardamom pods, toasted and lightly crushed

If you are a fan of syrup-based desserts, you will love this one, called *Ekmek Kadayif* in Turkish. I especially like the way the ricotta gives it a savory touch to balance out the sweetness. The cardamom is my addition, so not traditional; you could also try it with other spices, such as cloves, star anise, and cinnamon. You can find the dried bread-like sponge cake used in this recipe at Turkish supermarkets or bakeries—if they don't have it and you ask nicely, they will usually make it for you. Serve with ice cream or whipped cream.

Start by making the syrup. Put the water, sugar, and cardamom in a pan and bring to a boil. Reduce the heat and simmer to a light syrup consistency. Strain into a fresh pan once ready, and keep hot.

———

Meanwhile, place each cake half, cut side up, on 2 separate baking pans (the bottom half should go into a large baking pan that can sit over direct heat). Spoon the flower water, if using, over each half. Spread the ricotta over the bottom layer of the cake, and sprinkle with the walnuts. Top with the other cake.

———

Place the tray directly over medium heat and ladle the hot syrup over the cake bit by bit until all used up. Once the syrup has sunk to the bottom of the pan, use a tablespoon to keep basting it over until it is all absorbed. Leave to cool completely before cutting and serving.

POACHED & BARBECUED QUINCE

I first discovered that this was a great way to cook fruit when I tried it with peaches, so all types of stone fruit can be prepared like this too. Quince is very popular in Turkey: it is used in jams, compotes, or simply poached in syrup. My mom even likes it raw! This dish makes a lovely accompaniment to a piece of cake or tart, and is great served with ice cream and chopped pistachios, with some extra syrup poured over the top. But it also works well as a dessert on its own, especially after a barbecue.

SERVES 8

4¼ cups (1 liter) water
5 cups (2 lb 4 oz/1 kg) sugar
½ cinnamon stick
2 cloves
1 star anise
½ vanilla bean, halved
  lengthways and seeds
  scraped out
4 quinces
juice of 1 lemon
1 tablespoon orange blossom
  water (optional)
ice cream and chopped
  pistachios, to serve
  (optional)

Put the water in a pan with the sugar, cinnamon, cloves, star anise, vanilla seeds and pod, and bring to a boil. Simmer to reduce to a light syrup consistency.

Meanwhile, peel the quinces, cut them into quarters, remove the core, and rub the pieces with lemon juice. If your syrup is not ready to start poaching them immediately, put the quince in water with a squeeze of lemon juice.

Put the quince pieces in the syrup and simmer gently with a circle of parchment paper sitting directly on top of the liquid to hold the fruit down. Simmer for 8 minutes, then check to see if they are tender. You should be able to insert a knife or skewer comfortably. Don't overcook them, or they will turn to mush. Remove from the heat and leave to cool in the syrup. Add the orange blossom water, if using.

Heat a barbecue until ready to cook and the coals are grey, or heat a ridged grill pan until very hot. Drain the quince pieces and place on the hot barbecue or griddle pan. Cook for 2–3 minutes, or until charred, then turn and cook the other side. Dress the quince pieces in a little syrup before serving.

CANDIED BERGAMOT
& SEVILLE ORANGES

MAKES 40 PIECES

10 bergamot or Seville
oranges
1½ cups (350 ml) water
3¾ cups (1 lb 10 oz/750 g)
sugar
juice of ½ lemon

Preserving fruits and even some vegetables in syrup is very common in Turkish cooking. Cyprus is especially well known for producing the best preserves: I think this is because the produce is so incredible in the first place. Some of my favorites are whole green walnuts, and bergamot or Seville oranges (known in Turkish as *turunc*). Try using them in desserts to flavor creams, or even with some thick yogurt for breakfast. Traditionally, they are served on a small fork sitting inside a glass of cold water, to be eaten after a strong Turkish coffee.

Finely grate a thin layer of the zest off each fruit. Cut a small slice off the top and bottom, then slide the blade of a small knife between the pith and the flesh at the top and bottom of the fruit. Now score each orange 4 times from top to bottom, spacing the cuts evenly. Remove the 4 pieces of peel. Using a small knife, carefully remove most of the pith from inside each piece of peel.

———

To achieve a nice shape, roll up each piece of peel and pass a needle and strong cotton or string through it. Roll up the next piece and thread it onto the cotton next to the first one, pushing the

pieces close together. Repeat with the rest of the peel. Alternatively, you can just leave the pieces as they are. Once they are all threaded, tie up the ends tightly.

———

Place the peel pieces in a large bowl or pan of cold water and put a plate on top to hold them down. Change the water 2–3 times during the day and repeat this process for 4–5 days. (This is to remove the bitterness.)

———

Fill a large pan with fresh water, add the peel pieces, and bring to a boil. Drain and refill the pan, then bring to a boil again. Repeat this process 3 more times, then drain and leave to cool. Once they are cool enough to handle, take the peel pieces off the string.

———

Put the measured water in the pan, add the sugar, and bring it to a boil, then turn it down to a simmer and add the peel pieces. Cook for 30–40 minutes, or until the liquid takes on a loose, syrup-like consistency. Add the lemon juice. Remove from the heat, then transfer the peel and syrup to sterilized jars.

TAHINI SPIRAL & SPICED HOT CHOCOLATE

This is a take on the Spanish churros and hot chocolate. The crisp, flaky pastry goes perfectly with the gently spiced chocolate. You could try using peanut butter too. For me, a trip to a Turkish bakery normally involves picking up one of these spirals. For the hot chocolate, you could play around with the spices and use cumin, vanilla, chili, or baharat (see page 193).

In a large bowl, mix together the flour, yeast, sugar, and salt. Add the milk, butter, oil, and egg, bring it together with your hands, then knead to make a smooth dough. Cover the bowl with plastic wrap and set aside in a warm place until doubled in size (this will take about 1 hour).

___

Meanwhile, mix the tahini and sugar together. Once the dough has proofed, knead it gently and divide it into 4 equal pieces. Roll each piece into a ball and cover with a damp cloth. Preheat the oven to 400°F (200°C) and line a baking sheet with parchment paper.

___

Take one ball of dough and roll it out on a lightly floured surface into a circle about ¹/₈ in (3 mm) thick. Spread a quarter of the tahini mixture across the dough, leaving a ¾ in (2 cm) gap around the edge.

Sprinkle on a quarter of the walnuts, if using. Roll the dough up tightly to make a sausage shape. Take the ends of the dough and twist in opposite directions to make a corkscrew shape, then roll the whole thing into a spiral, tucking the end in underneath. Place it on the prepared baking sheet, pushing it down evenly to flatten it a little. Repeat with the rest of the dough. You might need to use 2 baking sheets to make sure you can leave a 1¼ in (3 cm) gap between each spiral. Let them rest for 15 minutes.

___

Brush the tops of the spirals with the eggwash. Scatter with the extra walnuts, if using. Bake for 25–30 minutes, or until golden and crisp.

___

To make the spiced hot chocolate, put the milk and spices in a saucepan over medium heat. Gently bring to a simmer, stirring occasionally. Turn the heat off and leave to infuse for 20 minutes. Add the chocolate and return to low heat until melted. Add as much sugar and orange blossom water as you wish. Strain out all the spices, pour the hot chocolate into cups, and grate over the nutmeg. Serve with the tahini spirals.

SERVES 4–8 (MAKES 4 LARGE SPIRALS)

8 cups (2 lb 4 oz/1 kg) all-purpose flour, plus extra for dusting

1 x ¼ oz (7 g) envelope instant dried yeast

1 tablespoon sugar

½ teaspoon fine salt

1 cup (250 ml) milk

3½ tablespoons (1¾ oz/50 g) unsalted butter, softened

3½ tablespoons sunflower oil

1 large egg

eggwash made from 1 large egg yolk beaten with 1 tablespoon milk

FOR THE FILLING

1 cup (9 oz/250 g) tahini

1¼ cups (9 oz/250 g) sugar

1½ cups (5½ oz/150 g) walnuts, toasted and crushed, plus extra for the tops (optional)

FOR THE SPICED HOT CHOCOLATE

6 cups (1.5 liters) milk

1 cinnamon stick, toasted

1 tablespoon fennel seeds, toasted

1 tablespoon coriander seeds, toasted

8 oz (225 g) dark chocolate (70% cocoa solids), chopped

sugar, to taste

orange blossom water, to taste (optional)

freshly grated nutmeg, to taste

INDEX

A

Adana köfte with pita bread 105
almonds: semolina cake 216
  spiced rice, apricot, almond & filo pie 151
apple tea: Cypriot 75 180
  Turkish apple tea 169
apricots (dried): pickled apricots 123
  spiced rice, apricot, almond & filo pie 151
artichoke & beef dolma 84
at-home ayran 170
ayran 170

B

bacon: pistachio-crusted banana & tahini
  French toast 42
  smoked bacon & Medjool date
  butter toasted sandwich 37
baharat 193
  baharat & chili-spiced fish börek 57
  baharat-spiced bread 46
  cheese, scallion, baharat & garlic
  böreks 55
  cuttlefish with baharat, peas &
  sea beans 120
  salad of baharat-roast duck 74
bananas: pistachio-crusted banana &
  tahini French toast 42
barbecued chicken wings 69
barley *see* pearl barley
beans: slow-cooked white beans with
  tomato, lemon & olive oil 143
beef: artichoke & beef dolma 84
  beef meatballs with sour cherry sauce 79
  çemen-braised short ribs 86
  fried beef & allspice köftes 93
  fried beef köfte 89
  şeftali 106
  spiced beef & bulgur köftes 90
  spiced beef & cheese sauce poğaças 56
  spiced braised oxtail with shallots 92
  steak tantuni 83

see also pastirma
bergamots: bergamot cream 215
  candied bergamots 227
black olive & pepper tapenade 189
black olive, hellim, onion & mint loaf 52
blood orange caramel 130
blood orange ganache 219
Bloody Mary, Turkish 175
böreks: baharat & chili-spiced fish
  börek 57
  cheese, scallion, baharat & garlic
  böreks 55
  semolina custard & filo börek 204
  spinach & feta börek 58
brandy: Cypriot 75 180
  Medjool date, espresso & fennel
  martini 179
bread: Adana köfte with pita bread 105
  baharat-spiced bread 46
  black olive, hellim, onion & mint
  loaf 52
  chicken livers with garlic, rosemary,
  cumin & date butter on toast 72
  pan-fried mackerel, black olive croute
  & tomato-pomegranate salad 129
  pistachio-crusted banana & tahini
  French toast 42
  smoked bacon & Medjool date
  butter toasted sandwich 37
  spicy tomato & bread sauce 34
  steak tantuni 83
  tomato, raw onion, purslane, crisp
  bread & mint salad 15
breadcrumbs: brown butter bread
  sauce 86
  çemen crumbs 39
  fried beef köfte 89
  za'atar crumbs 78
brown shrimp kaygana 39
brunch, Oklava 30–43
bulgur: bulgur pilav 79

  spiced beef & bulgur köftes 90
  spicy red lentil köftes 138
buns: spiced beef & cheese sauce
  poğaças 56
butter: chili butter 186
  Medjool date butter 186
buttered freekeh with chickpeas, green
  olives, currants & pistachios 159

C

cabbage: pickled red cabbage 198
  ricotta dumplings 154
  spiced chickpeas, buttered cabbage,
  poached duck egg & tulum cheese 140
  vegetable dolmas 152
cakes: semolina cake 216
  syrup sponge cake stuffed with ricotta
  & walnuts 223
  trilece cake 208
candied bergamots & Seville oranges 227
candied lime zest 207
caper dressing 194
caper leaves: fried red mullet, pickled
  apricots & caper leaves 123
caramel: blood orange caramel 130
  caramelized pineapple 207
  chocolate, prune & cardamom
  delice 212
  dark chocolate & praline katmer 211
  sherry vinegar caramel 195
  spiced rice pudding brûlée 207
  trilece cake 208
cauliflower, chili-roasted 136
çay, traditional Turkish 166
çemen 199
  çemen-braised short ribs 86
  çemen crumbs 39
  crispy fried scallions, cheese
  sauce & çemen crumbs 150
cheese: baked lamb-fat potatoes, fried
  duck egg, grilled hellim & sherry

vinegar caramel 146

black olive, hellim, onion & mint loaf 52

brown shrimp kaygana 39

cheese sauce pide with charred leeks & crispy potatoes 65

cheese, scallion, baharat & garlic böreks 55

chicken & garlic köfte pide 63

crispy fried scallions, cheese sauce & çemen crumbs 150

feta, garlic & poppyseed crisps 26

pilavuna 49

Romaine lettuce salad 18

salad of baharat-roast duck with feta 74

sour cherry pearl barley, crispy kale, yogurt, chili butter & sheep's cheese 157

spiced beef & cheese sauce poğaças 56

spiced chickpeas, buttered cabbage, poached duck egg & tulum cheese 140

spinach & feta börek 58

whipped feta 190

zucchini, feta & mint fritters 24

see also ricotta

cherries: beef meatballs with sour cherry sauce 79

sour cherry pearl barley, crispy kale, yogurt, chili butter & sheep's cheese 157

chicken: barbecued chicken wings 69

chicken & garlic köfte pide 63

chicken kebabs 102

chicken livers with garlic, rosemary, cumin & date butter on toast 72

chili-garlic glazed chicken 78

Circassian chicken 29

chickpeas: buttered freekeh with chickpeas, green olives, currants & pistachios 159

Mom's hummus 110

spiced chickpeas, buttered cabbage, poached duck egg & tulum cheese 140

chili: baharat & chili-spiced fish börek 57

chili butter 186

chili-garlic glazed chicken 78

chili-roasted cauliflower 136

fried dried chili yogurt 199

spicy tomato & bread sauce 34

Urfa chili dressing 130

Urfa chili mayonnaise 188

chocolate: blood orange ganache 219

chocolate, prune & cardamom delice 212

dark chocolate & praline katmer 211

spiced hot chocolate 228

Circassian chicken 29

cod, pistachio-crusted 125

coffee: Medjool date, espresso & fennel martini 179

Turkish coffee 172

corn, barbecued 144

cream: blood orange ganache 219

chocolate, prune & cardamom delice 212

orange cream 200

crepes: brown shrimp kaygana 39

crisps: feta, garlic & poppyseed 26

cucumber: salad of Romano beans, cucumber, fennel & kale 21

currants: buttered freekeh with chickpeas, green olives, currants & pistachios 159

cuttlefish with baharat, peas & sea beans 120

Cypriot pastirma & broken eggs 34

Cypriot 75 180

Cyprus potato salad 113

D

date night menu 133

dates: chicken livers with garlic, rosemary, cumin & date butter on toast 72

Medjool date butter 186

Medjool date, espresso & fennel martini 179

smoked bacon & Medjool date

butter toasted sandwich 37

dinner party menu 132

dolmas: artichoke & beef dolma 84

vegetable dolma 152

dressings: caper dressing 194

feta dressing 18

pomegranate dressing 126, 195

sumac dressing 194

Urfa chili dressing 130

yogurt dressing 23

drinks: at-home ayran 170

Cypriot 75 180

homemade limonata 164

Medjool date, espresso & fennel martini 179

pomegranate & sumac martini 176

pomegranate tea 164

rakı 183

spiced hot chocolate 228

traditional Turkish çay 166

Turkish apple tea 169

Turkish Bloody Mary 175

Turkish coffee 172

duck: salad of baharat-roast duck 74

duck eggs: baked lamb-fat potatoes, fried duck egg, grilled hellim & sherry vinegar caramel 146

spiced chickpeas, buttered cabbage, poached duck egg & tulum cheese 140

dumplings, ricotta 154

E

eggs: baked lamb-fat potatoes, fried duck egg, grilled hellim & sherry vinegar caramel 146

brown shrimp kaygana 39

Cypriot pastirma & broken eggs 34

menemen 40

spiced chickpeas, buttered cabbage, poached duck egg & tulum cheese 140

eggplants: fried vegetables with garlic yogurt & pomegranate 23

F

fennel: salad of Romano beans, cucumber, fennel & kale 21

fennel (ground): fennel yogurt 79

fennel seeds: Medjool date, espresso & fennel martini 179

fenugreek (ground): çemen 199

feta dressing 18

feta, garlic & poppyseed crisps 26

figs: salad of baharat-roast duck with poached figs 74

filo pastry: baharat & chili-spiced fish börek 57

dark chocolate & praline katmer 211

feta, garlic & poppyseed crisps 26

filo shards 219

semolina custard & filo börek 204

spiced rice, apricot, almond & filo pie 151

spinach & feta börek 58

fish: baharat & chili-spiced fish börek 57

see also cod, monkfish, etc.

freekeh: buttered freekeh with chickpeas, green olives, currants & pistachios 159

French toast, pistachio-crusted banana & tahini 42

fritters: crispy fried scallions 150

fried mussels 116

rabbit fritters 95

zucchini, feta & mint fritters 24

G

ganache, blood orange 219

garlic: çemen 199

cheese, scallion, baharat & garlic böreks 55

feta, garlic & poppyseed crisps 26

fried vegetables with garlic yogurt & pomegranate 23

H

hake: seafood vermicelli with mussels, hake & shrimp 119

hollandaise, preserved lemon 39

hummus, Mom's 110

J

jello: muhallebi with strawberry jello 220

rum jello 207

K

kadayif, ricotta & vanilla 215

kale: salad of Romano beans, cucumber, fennel & kale 21

sour cherry pearl barley, crispy kale, yogurt, chili butter & sheep's cheese 157

katmer, dark chocolate & praline 211

kaygana, brown shrimp 39

kebabs: Adana köfte 105

chicken pieces 102

lamb chop kebabs 102

lamb shish kebabs 102

şeftali 106

köfte pide, chicken & garlic 63

köftes: Adana köfte 105

fried beef & allspice köftes 93

fried beef köfte 89

spiced beef & bulgur köftes 90

spicy red lentil köftes 138

L

lamb: Adana köfte 105

crispy pomegranate-glazed lamb breast 96

lamb chop kebabs 102

lamb shish kebabs 102

quince & rosemary-glazed lamb 99

lamb fat: baked lamb-fat potatoes 146

lamb caul fat: şeftali 106

lamb suet: şeftali 106

lamb's liver, spiced fried crispy 101

leeks: cheese sauce pide with charred leeks & crispy potatoes 65

lemon: homemade limonata 164

pistachio-crusted cod with preserved lemon butter sauce 125

preserved lemon hollandaise 39

preserved lemons 201

lentils: spicy red lentil köftes 138

lettuce: Cyprus potato salad with Romaine lettuce 113

Romaine lettuce salad with candied walnuts & feta dressing 18

spicy red lentil köftes with lettuce 138

limes: candied lime zest 207

lime mayonnaise 188

limonata 164

liver: chicken livers with garlic, rosemary, cumin & date butter on toast 72

spiced fried crispy lamb's liver 101

lychees, marinated 207

M

mackerel: pan-fried mackerel, black olive croute & tomato-pomegranate salad 129

marinated olives 196

martini: Medjool date, espresso & fennel martini 179

pomegranate & sumac martini 176

mascarpone: bergamot cream 215

mayonnaise: lime mayonnaise 188

Urfa chili mayonnaise 188

meatballs: beef meatballs with sour cherry sauce 79

fried beef & allspice köftes 93

fried beef köfte 89

Medjool date butter 186

Medjool date, espresso & fennel martini 179

menemen 40

menus: date night 133

dinner party 132

party 160

milk: muhallebi 220
spiced hot chocolate 228
mint: mint oil 154
tarama with fried mussels & mint
oil 116
tomato, raw onion, purslane, crisp
bread & mint salad 15
zucchini, feta & mint fritters 24
monkfish, citrus, Urfa Chili dressing &
cilantro 130
muhallebi with strawberry jello 220
muhammara 190
Mom's hummus 110
Mom's pilav 110
mussels: seafood vermicelli with
mussels, hake & shrimp 119
tarama with fried mussels & mint
oil 116

N

nuts see pistachios, walnuts, etc.

O

octopus: braised octopus pide 64
oil, mint 154
Oklava brunch 30–43
olives: black olive & pepper tapenade 189
black olive, hellim, onion & mint loaf 52
braised octopus pide 64
buttered freekeh with chickpeas, green
olives, currants & pistachios 159
marinated olives 196
pan-fried mackerel, black olive croute
& tomato-pomegranate salad 129
onions: onion salad 80
red onion, pepper & parsley salad 83
salad of baharat-roast duck with
sumac onions 74
şeftali 106
shepherd's salad 113
tomato, raw onion, purslane, crisp
bread & mint salad 15
orange blossom syrup 200

oranges: blood orange caramel 130
blood orange ganache 219
candied Seville oranges 227
orange cream 200
oxtail: spiced braised oxtail with
shallots 92

P

palm sugar: chili-garlic glazed chicken 78
grilled quails with a palm sugar, sumac
& oregano glaze 76
paprika: çemen 199
parsley: şeftali 106
tomato-pomegranate salad with
parsley 16
party menu 160
pastirma: barbecued chicken wings with
garlic & Kayseri pastirma dressing 69
Cypriot pastirma & broken eggs 34
pastries: baharat & chili-spiced fish
börek 57
cheese sauce pide with charred leeks &
crispy potatoes 65
cheese, scallion, baharat & garlic
böreks 55
chicken & garlic köfte pide 63
dark chocolate & praline katmer 211
feta, garlic & poppyseed crisps 26
pides 60
pilavuna 49
ricotta & vanilla kadayif 215
semolina custard & filo börek 204
spiced rice, apricot, almond & filo
pie 151
spinach & feta börek 58
tahini spiral 228
pear, poached 219
pearl barley: sour cherry pearl barley,
crispy kale, yogurt, chili butter &
sheep's cheese 157
peas: cuttlefish with baharat, peas & sea
beans 120
peppers: baked lamb-fat potatoes, fried

duck egg, grilled hellim & sherry
vinegar caramel 146
fried vegetables with garlic yogurt &
pomegranate 23
menemen 40
red onion, pepper & parsley
salad 83
sivri biber relish 80
smoked salsa 63
pickles: lime pickle 188
pickled apricots 123
pickled red cabbage 198
pides 60
braised octopus pide 64
cheese sauce pide with charred leeks
& crispy potatoes 65
chicken & garlic köfte pide 63
pilav: bulgur pilav 79
Mom's pilav 110
pilavuna 49
pine nuts, ricotta dumplings with 154
pineapple, caramelized 207
pistachios: buttered freekeh with
chickpeas, green olives, currants
& pistachios 159
dark chocolate & praline katmer 211
pistachio-crusted banana & tahini
French toast 42
pistachio-crusted cod 125
spiced rice pudding brûlée 207
pita bread, Adana köfte with 105
poğaças, spiced beef & cheese sauce 56
pomegranate juice: pomegranate &
sumac martini 176
pomegranate tea 164
pomegranate molasses: crispy
pomegranate-glazed lamb 96
pomegranate dressing 126, 195
tomato-pomegranate salad 16, 129
tomato-pomegranate salsa 34
pomegranate seeds: fried vegetables
with garlic yogurt & pomegranate 23
pomegranate dressing 126

poppyseeds: feta, garlic & poppyseed crisps 26

potatoes: baked lamb-fat potatoes 146

cheese sauce pide with charred leeks & crispy potatoes 65

Cyprus potato salad 113

fried beef köfte 89

praline: chocolate, prune & cardamom delice 212

dark chocolate & praline katmer 211

preserved lemons 201

preserved lemon butter sauce 125

preserved lemon hollandaise 39

prunes: chocolate, prune & cardamom delice 212

purslane: tomato, raw onion, purslane, crisp bread & mint salad 15

Q

quails with a palm sugar, sumac & oregano glaze 76

quince: poached & barbecued quince 224

quince & rosemary-glazed lamb 99

R

rabbit fritters 95

rakı 183

red cabbage, pickled 198

red mullet, pickled apricots & caper leaves 123

relishes: sivri biber relish 80

tomato relish 189

rice: artichoke & beef dolma 84

Mom's pilav 110

spiced rice, apricot, almond & filo pie 151

spiced rice pudding brûlée 207

vegetable dolmas 152

ricotta: braised octopus pide 64

ricotta & vanilla kadayif 215

ricotta dumplings 154

syrup sponge cake stuffed with ricotta & walnuts 223

roes: tarama with fried mussels & mint oil 116

Romaine lettuce salad 18

Romano beans: salad of Romano beans, cucumber, fennel & kale 21

rum: pomegranate & sumac martini 176

rum jello 207

S

salads: baharat-roast duck with feta, sumac onions, poached figs & salted walnuts 74

Cyprus potato salad 113

fried vegetables with garlic yogurt & pomegranate 23

onion salad 80

red onion, pepper & parsley salad 83

Romaine lettuce salad 18

Romano beans, cucumber, fennel & kale 21

shepherd's salad 113

tomato-pomegranate salad 16, 129

tomato, raw onion, purslane, crisp bread & mint salad 15

salsas: smoked salsa 63

tomato-pomegranate salsa 34

salt: preserved lemons 201

salted walnuts 74

sandwiches: smoked bacon & Medjool date butter toasted sandwich 37

steak tantuni 83

sauces: brown butter bread sauce 86

cheese sauce 56, 65

preserved lemon butter sauce 125

preserved lemon hollandaise 39

spicy tomato & bread sauce 34

yogurt sauce 154

sausages: şeftali 106

sea bass with caramelized shallot purée & pomegranate dressing 126

scallions: cheese, scallion, baharat & garlic böreks 55

crispy fried scallions, cheese

sauce & çemen crumbs 150

spicy red lentil köftes with lettuce, scallions & lemon 138

sea beans: cuttlefish with baharat, peas & sea beans 120

seafood vermicelli with mussels, hake & shrimp 119

şeftali 106

semolina: semolina cake 216

semolina custard & filo börek 204

sesame seeds: pilavuna 49

spiced beef & cheese sauce poğaças 56

za'atar crumbs 78

shallots: caramelized shallot purée 126

spiced braised oxtail with shallots 92

shepherd's salad 113

sherry vinegar caramel 195

shrimp: brown shrimp kaygana 39

seafood vermicelli with mussels, hake & shrimp 119

sivri biber relish 80

smoked cod roe: tarama with fried mussels & mint oil 116

smoked bacon & Medjool date butter toasted sandwich 37

smoked salsa 63

sour cherry pearl barley, crispy kale, yogurt, chili butter & sheep's cheese 157

spice mixes: baharat 193

çemen 199

spinach & feta börek 58

steak tantuni 83

stews: spiced braised oxtail with shallots 92

strawberries: muhallebi with strawberry jello 220

ricotta & vanilla kadayif with bergamot cream & strawberries 215

suet: şeftali 106

sumac: barbecued corn 144

grilled quails with a palm sugar, sumac & oregano glaze 76

pomegranate & sumac martini 176
salad of baharat-roast duck with
  sumac onions 74
sumac dressing 194
syrup, orange blossom 200
syrup sponge cake stuffed with ricotta &
  walnuts 223

T
tahini: Mom's hummus 110
  pistachio-crusted banana & tahini
    French toast 42
  tahini spiral 228
tapenade, black olive & pepper 189
tarama with fried mussels & mint oil 116
tea: pomegranate tea 164
  traditional Turkish çay 166
  Turkish apple tea 169
toast: chicken livers with garlic,
  rosemary, cumin & date butter
    on toast 72
  pistachio-crusted banana & tahini
    French toast 42
  smoked bacon & Medjool date
    butter toasted sandwich 37
tomatoes: artichoke & beef dolma 84
  bulgur pilav 79
  menemen 40
  salad of Romano beans, cucumber,
    fennel & kale 21
  shepherd's salad 113
  slow-cooked white beans with tomato,
    lemon & olive oil 143
  smoked salsa 63
  spicy tomato & bread sauce 34
  tomato-pomegranate salad 16, 129
  tomato-pomegranate salsa 34
  tomato, raw onion, purslane, crisp
    bread & mint salad 15
  tomato relish 189
  Turkish Bloody Mary 175
  vegetable dolmas 152
trilece cake 208

Turkish apple tea 169
Turkish Bloody Mary 175
Turkish coffee 172
Turkish peppers *see* peppers
turnip juice: pomegranate dressing 195

U
Urfa chili dressing 130
Urfa chili mayonnaise 188

V
veal shish 80
vegetable dolmas 152
vermicelli: Mom's pilav 110
  seafood vermicelli with mussels,
    hake & shrimp 119
vinegar: sherry vinegar caramel 195
vodka: Medjool date, espresso & fennel
  martini 179
  pomegranate & sumac martini 176
  Turkish Bloody Mary 175

W
walnuts: chicken & garlic köfte pide 63
  Circassian chicken 29
  muhammara 190
  Romaine lettuce salad with candied
    walnuts 18
  salted walnuts 74
  syrup sponge cake stuffed with ricotta
    & walnuts 223
  tahini spiral 228
whipped feta 190
white beans: slow-cooked white beans
  with tomato, lemon & olive oil 143
wine: Cypriot 75 180
  poached pear 219
  spiced braised oxtail with shallots 92

Y
yogurt: at-home ayran 170
  crispy pomegranate-glazed lamb
    breast with yogurt 96

fennel yogurt 79
fried dried chili yogurt 199
sour cherry pearl barley, crispy kale,
  yogurt, chili butter & sheep's
  cheese 157
yogurt dressing 23
yogurt sauce 154

Z
za'atar: barbecued corn with sumac,
  garlic, lemon butter & za'atar 144
  za'atar crumbs 78
zucchinis: zucchini, feta & mint fritters 24
  fried vegetables with garlic yogurt &
    pomegranate 23

ACKNOWLEDGMENTS

Selin

The hospitality industry is a notoriously difficult one to work in, but it is also full of people with an enormous amount of passion and kindness. On the road to opening Oklava, a huge number of people helped us in various ways, generous with their time and expertise. It is incredibly humbling to think that so many people helped because they wanted us to succeed—thank you to all of you.

I have to specifically name some of them here though, for all of their help. So first of all I would like to thank all past and present team members at Oklava: you guys have been amazing and all worked so hard to create our beautiful little restaurant, and make mine and Laura's dream a reality.

Lucy, for always sticking by me. You were there with me from Kopapa to the pop-ups and from day one at Oklava. Your hard work and dedication make you an incredible chef and I am so proud of you.

Nick, my super sous chef, I cannot thank you enough: this book would not have materialized if not for all your hard work and many, many hours spent in the kitchen covering me. Thank you for never getting annoyed by the fact that I would sit at the bar writing this book and boss you about at the same time! I am truly honored to have you work by my side and I couldn't do this without you.

Laura, you are an amazing business partner and I couldn't have imagined anyone better to work alongside me.

Vince Cottam, my college mentor, you kickstarted so many opportunities for me and have always believed in me.

Peter Gordon and Michael McGrath, working at The Providores was a magical time in my life, and I feel so fortunate to have worked in your restaurant. Peter, cooking in your kitchen, where I was encouraged to experiment and cook freely, has shaped me into the chef I am today. You are my hero.

Hannah Norris, you have believed in me from day one. Thank you for championing me and my cooking.

Zoe Ross for being a great support.

Chris Terry, our photographer, his assistant Danny, and Cynthia Inions our prop stylist, for coming out to Cyprus to shoot all the gorgeous photos and help shape the Oklava book.

Mum, for supporting my career, inspiring so many of the recipes, and coming out to Cyprus for the photo shoot to help me cook all the recipes. My sisters Sinem and Sibel, for

convincing my parents it was OK for me to be a chef, and to my nieces and nephew Kayla, Joshan, and Ella for being so incredibly excited about everything I do.

All of my friends, but especially Tamara, Asya, Gabby, Harshini, Ruyan, Sophie, and Danielle, for your encouragement and putting up with the fact you don't see me very much as I'm always working.

Everyone at Octopus, especially Stephanie Jackson for trusting that I could write this book; I'm not quite sure why she was so convinced I could do this but her gentle powers of persuasion certainly worked. Yasia Williams for totally understanding the Oklava vision and ethos and translating it into the book, and Alex Stetter for being an incredibly patient editor.

Finally, most of all I would like to thank Rebecca. You have been through this whole journey with me, supported me through highs and lows, and always kept me believing that Oklava would be a reality. I am eternally grateful to you for simply always being there and never giving up on me.

Laura

First and foremost I would like to thank my wonderful Mom and Dad, without whose never-ending support and encouragement I would not have had the courage to take this exciting journey with Selin. Thank you also to my sister Hannah and my loyal friends, who know who they are and have all done their bit to make Oklava a reality.

I will second Selin's thank yous, in particular a big thanks to our fantastic staff. Matt, Elisa, and Steph have done a wonderful job of supporting me through our exciting first year and some of the brilliant (if we do say so ourselves) drinks recipes in this book would not be there without them. Thanks to all those in the industry who have helped both guide my career and make our dream of Oklava happen, particularly all those at Salt Yard Group, where I spent five happy years prior and learned a huge amount.

Thanks of course to Selin herself for being such a uniquely talented business partner and to her family, who welcomed us so warmly in Cyprus—particularly her grandparents and her mom Pervin, who has changed my idea of packing a suitcase well forever.

Finally a mention for my little Ollie, who I was pregnant with during our opening and when writing this book. Thank you for inspiring me to keep pushing forwards and pursuing this dream, I only hope to make you proud.